The Better Water Gardens Book of

Patio
Ponds

Gordon T. Ledbetter

The Better Water Gardens Book of

Patio
Ponds

BWG, Blagdon, Avon

This book was designed and produced by
Alphabet and Image Ltd., Sherborne, Dorset,
England.

First published in England in 1982 by
Better Water Gardens,
Blagdon, Avon, England.

ISBN 0 9507982 0 7

Line drawings by Peter Haillay.

Photoset by Photosetting & Secretarial Services Ltd., Yeovil, Somerset
Printed and bound by Butler & Tanner Ltd., Frome, Somerset, England

Contents

Acknowledgements

While writing this book I obtained advice and help from many people. In particular I should like to thank Tom Conroy of Irish Cement Ltd, for giving me the benefit of his expert advice relating to concrete and paving. I should also like to thank Adrian and Valerie Beatty, Anthony and Wendy Berry, Eileen and George De Long, Michael Dover, Cecil Dunbar, Rosemary ffolliott, Philip Goor, David Gould, Jim Horan, Eamonn Hughes, Eddie O'Connor, Mary Crain Penniman, David Proger and Jim Ryan, who all provided generous help. My thanks are also due to Tony Birks-Hay who exercised his skill as a potter and presented me with two splendid fountain masks representing Comedy and Tragedy. Without specifying which, friends tell me one of them bears a striking resemblance to myself. Leslie Birks-Hay kindly undertook the strenuous tasks of editing and indexing the text for which I am most thankful.

To those who gave me permission to photograph their fine patio ponds I am most grateful: Bill Foley, Maria José Fonseca, Mrs C. J. Fox, Andrew Ganly and Derek Noble Johnston, Sir Frederick Gibberd and Peter Holloway. I should also like to express my appreciation of R.H.S. Wisley and the National Botanic Gardens, Dublin; as well as Blagdon Water Gardens, Irish Butyl Ltd, Emboss Ireland Ltd, Marlfield Nurseries and Northern Brick Redlands.

Finally, I wish to thank my sister, Audrey Baker, for reading the script and providing much useful criticism and many suggestions.

G.T.L.
Co. Wicklow, Ireland.

1 Patios, ponds and statuary

There is a character in John Steinbeck's novel *The Winter of our Discontent* called Joey, who exclaims how he intends spending the Fourth of July holiday. He says: 'I'm going to New York and get a room at an hotel and I'm going to watch the waterfall across Times Square for two solid days with my shoes off.' That is Joey's idea of bliss. I suppose it is most people's idea of bliss. Water foaming, boiling, swirling over waterfalls or spouting forth from fountains, breaking into incandescent particles, these sights affect us all; as surely as a pond, a stretch of placid water, supporting a peaceful water-lily, reflecting the images of surrounding plants and flowers. Poor Joey, he was no gardener, he could hardly have known that water-lilies and water plants are very easy to grow. Nor could he have known that a fountain, no matter how large or small, is a simple thing to install. Like many another person, Joey was probably under the illusion that a pond and lilies require a great deal of space. In actual fact the area you can enclose with your arms is quite large enough to support one of the miniature water-lilies and several marginal plants as well.

Imagine, for example, a small garden featuring a muddy patch of ill-kept grass with perhaps a ragged shrub or two stuck in a corner. If you ever catch a commuter train through the suburbs of a large town, in the temperate regions, you will pass a thousand such sad-looking gardens. If you were to approach the owner of such a patch, he would be almost certain to remark that it is just not possible to make anything of so small an area. The grass becomes worn from over-use, there is after all nowhere else to walk; and, besides, the rain inevitably turns the grass into a muddy patch in winter. Equally easy to imagine is the backyard where the problem is not too much rain but too little and too much sun, as in Mediterranean areas, as well as Australia and much of America. The backyard, without constant care, turns into a dusty, miniature desert. Water restrictions may add to the problem. Apart from an occasional tough-looking cactus, the backyard is often left to look after itself. The result is no garden at all.

Apart from the problems of climate (there is in any case no such thing as perfect weather conditions anywhere), many people are away from home for lengthy periods. Many more simply do not want to give up the time necessary to maintain a conventional garden of lawns and flower beds. For better or for worse, the way many of us lead our lives today, there is not time to spend on garden chores such as weeding and mowing; or to put it another way, we are not prepared to give up the time to these chores. But what I think most people who are in any way interested in gardening are prepared to do is *occasional* maintenance work, when they have time to do it. Being tied down to regular work, which if not carried out at the right time means the garden turns into a wilder-

A small pond which entirely fills the width of a limited space, with access to either end gained by stepping stones. Note also the fountain made by drilling a large rock sited in the pond – a very conspicuous focal point. Gravel is attractive visually but should be avoided as a paving material where a lot of foot traffic is likely.

ness, is what most people would want to avoid.

If this is how you feel about gardening, then a patio water garden offers an attractive option. A patio (especially if laid on concrete) and a fountain require hardly any maintenance at all. Shrubs, when grown in tubs, pots and small raised beds, require the minimum of weeding and are readily watered. Incidentally, the dictionary definition of a patio is 'a roofless inner courtyard'. But in modern usage and in the building trade the term patio is used to describe any area given over to paving slabs. Usually, for reasons discussed later, the patio is partially or completely surrounded by walls and is usually set next to the house.

A pond perhaps needs less looking after than any other feature of a garden. Water-lilies can be left undisturbed for years, while marginal or moisture-loving plants, paradoxically, are probably less susceptible to drought than plants in a bed or border. Moisture-loving plants are well adapted to the rise and fall of the water-level. Just provided their roots can always reach water they are satisfied. Hot weather dries out raised beds long before it has any appreciable effect on a pond. (The leaves of water-lilies floating on the surface of the water actually reduce evaporation.) So water shortage should not put you off installing a pond. If you have young children and toddlers it is a different question. Even a small pond, let it be emphasised, is a real hazard to the very young. If you have a young family, put in a fountain statue (with an underground reservoir if necessary) and avoid danger (see page 28). Alternatively, keep the pond size at a play area or sandpit until your children reach a safe age.

A pond or fountain is probably the most dominant feature that a garden can possess. Indeed a patio (even one with few plants) *becomes* a garden simply by the presence of water. Even those with little or no interest in gardening, you will find, immediately turn to the pond. Children and adults are alike in this respect; water is irresistible to almost all of us. A pond legitimises a patio in a way that I think no other feature can. You can sit round a pond, drink by it, eat by it. The same can hardly be said about a rose border or shrub. So the subject of this book is the design and construction of the patio water garden, a form of garden well suited to so many of those dreary backyards, neglected and forsaken, that I spoke of earlier.

These then, in a nutshell, are the practical advantages to be gained from a patio pond garden. But I can hear some objections being raised. In the first place you might feel that a garden made up entirely of concrete paving slabs or tiles or bricks has a dreary sameness about it, that it lacks the constant changing quality of a garden filled with borders. Such criticism reminds me of a passage in Arthur Rubinstein's autobiography *My Many Years*. Watching Picasso painting the same scene again and again Rubinstein questioned the artist: '"Are you painting this subject on commission? Is there a great demand for it?" He looked at me with dismay. "What a

stupid question", he said. "Every minute there is another light, every day is different too, so whatever I paint becomes always a new subject."' In a sense the apparently unchanging materials of a well designed patio garden are never quite the same two days running. Bricks, stone, tiles or whatever do reflect the different light of different days as well as the change in the seasons. But in any case, no one is likely to want to build a patio without also growing plants in and around it. It is the plants which provide the whole area with its soul, with a sense of the garden being a living, changing thing. Even evergreens like Juniper and heathers and Bay (all excellent subjects for the patio), which on casual acquaintance appear static, change with each season. Their growth is quite apparent in spring, when bright green or blue shoots emerge, in the summer they change again and in autumn too. In winter when most other things have turned to decay, evergreens remain stately, standing like sentinels in the mist or fading light of a winter day. You will notice too such things as dewdrops upon their spreading branches, and the sight of snow spread over their horizontal boughs, and dappled shade through swaying branches. No, a patio pond garden, as surely as any other, reflects the cycle of nature. It is never static, never remains the same. It is a garden for all seasons.

As with any kind of construction, the design of a pond and patio will, to some extent, be influenced by the materials used and the kind of patio and pond that you wish to construct. Design is a topic on its own, dealt with in Chapter 11, but we begin with the alternative ways of *making* a pond.

Children adore water – as their faces always show – but supervision is necessary where toddlers and very young children are concerned.

A well planted glass-fibre pond, with raised bed and ornamental water feature. Note how carefully the banks of the pond have been levelled.

Making the pond

There are basically three different ways of making a pond. You could choose a rigid or semi-rigid glass-fibre or plastic pool such as can be bought at many garden centres. As the shape of these pools is pre-determined, all that is required is to excavate your site so that it conforms as closely as possible to the shape of the pool. Then line the site with damp sand or peat and bed the pool down. Having the sand or peat damp will make it adhere to the banks if they are sloped. If they are vertical then you may be able to ease in some sand between the bank and the pool as you lower the pool into place. Avoid, as far as possible, leaving gaps under or around the pool. Usually, moulded pools can be laid in place quickly and easily. Moreover, glass-fibre and plastic are tough and almost indestructible. As against that, pre-formed pools are more expensive than most other types, and you might regard the fact that the dimensions are already decided as something of a disadvantage. It means, of course, that you cannot make the pond to your own design. If you do choose a moulded pool, make sure it is at least 45 cm deep. Anything less limits the kind of hardy lilies you can grow; but much more important is the fact that there is a relationship between the depth of a pond and the clarity of the water it contains (this is discussed in Chapter 7).

Probably more ponds are being made today by using what are known as pond liners than by all other methods put together. They have many virtues. They are comparatively cheap and are easy to install. The fact that they are flexible means that they will fit any shape of pond. Nor is there any limitation with regard to size. Liners can be made up to any size and to any desired dimensions. Like moulded pools, pond liners are easily obtainable from garden centres and aquatic specialists. Scientific research is continually producing new recipes for pond liners, often as a spin-off from industrial research concerning roofing material, reservoirs, canal lining and the like.

Basically, pond liners are made from plastic (Polyethylene, or polythene as it is

A formal glass-fibre pond ready for setting in an excavation. This particular pond has a perimeter shelf for marginal baskets, a useful feature.

more commonly known, is a type of plastic); Polyvinyl Chloride, or PVC, which is a quite different material; and the finest lining material for ponds, Butyl rubber.

In choosing a liner the points to be borne in mind are the toughness of the material: how susceptible it may be to tearing, cracking or puncturing; but above all, how vulnerable it may be to the ultra-violet rays of the sun. The area of the liner below water level is relatively safe from the sun's rays, but above the water line the ultra-violet rays of the sun can wreak havoc. Some liners become brittle when exposed to sunlight, and they then tend to crack and disintegrate.

Polythene is the cheapest material for lining a pond, but it is also the one most easily damaged by sunlight. Black polythene, the thicker the better, is more resilient than clear polythene. But as the water level in any pond is bound to fall from time to time, due to evaporation, the sides of the pond will be exposed directly to the sun. This is likely to take place most often during the summer when the sun is most potent. Without taking preventative measures, a polythene liner might last only a few seasons. But its life can be greatly extended by completely shielding the sides of the pond from the sun. This is most easily done by cutting out a ledge to the depth of one or more bricks or other building material, around the top of the sides. After the liner has been laid, the bricks are placed on this ledge, securing them with mortar if desired. Not only will the bricks provide the polythene with the necessary protection, but they are an attractive feature. There is no reason why bricks should not be used with other materials as well. Another point regarding polythene is how easily it can be punctured, and it is a difficult material to repair satisfactorily. The best method is to put over the puncture a piece of double-sided tape, several lengths side by side, in fact, so as to make up a square of the tape. Then place a patch of polythene over the tape. Finally secure the patch the whole way round with

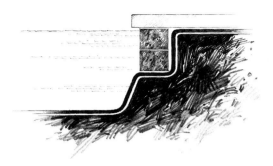

Fig. 1. Means of protecting a liner from the direct rays of the sun by having bricks set on a shelf.

single-sided tape. To have any chance of succeeding with the repair, the polythene must be scrupulously clean and absolutely dry.

PVC or Polyvinyl Chloride, although it looks very similar to polythene, has, in fact, quite different characteristics. In the first place ultra-violet rays have comparatively little effect upon PVC, which can be expected to last many years if treated with reasonable respect. It is also, to a limited extent, stretchable which polythene is not. PVC comes in different grades. For pond use, the best consists of two layers of PVC containing a weave of nylon. This laminated form is more durable than a single sheet. PVC is readily repaired and suppliers usually stock repair kits.

But without doubt, the best of all pond liners is Butyl rubber, which is available in thicknesses ranging from 0.75 mm to 2 mm. Butyl 1 mm thick is what is normally used in pond construction. The material was first used by the United States army in the Pacific during the Second World War for the transport and storage of water. It has since been used in countless domestic and in-dustrial situations, as well as for ponds. It is very tough (easily repaired if punctured), very elastic, and extensive tests show that sunlight has virtually no effect on its strength at all. While Butyl rubber is about twice the price of plain PVC, and perhaps 15 per cent more expensive than laminated PVC, there is no comparison as regards longevity or durability.

Having excavated the site, but before laying the liner, make absolutely certain that the banks are the same level the whole way round. Nothing looks worse than a lop-sided pond. Place a straight plank across the banks and place a builder's level on top of the plank. Add or subtract soil around the perimeter, taking readings as you go. The best method is to start with two readings: first the length of the pond and then the width. Having satisfied yourself that the pond is level in these respects, place the plank diagonally across the pond at a variety of angles. You may find some variation from your first readings. Incidentally, it is worth checking that your level is in order before beginning. Lay the level on a table or other flat surface until you find one which places the bubble right in the centre, between the two markings. Then reverse the level on exactly the same spot. If the level is in working order the bubble should return to the middle once again. If your site is too wide or long for a single plank there is another

Levelling the banks of a pond by means of a straight edge (a plank of wood having parallel sides) and a builder's level. If the straight edge does not reach right across the pond, then use a datum peg set in the pond as shown below.

Having removed all sharp stones, it is well worth while laying down a few centimetres of sand – a 'blinding' – on the base, before installing the liner.

method of getting the banks level. In the centre of the pond drive in a stake with a wooden mallet. Place one end of the board on the bank and the other end on top of the stake. Hammer down the stake until you get a level reading. Then, by moving the board along the banks in a sweeping, circular fashion the rest of the banks can be adjusted.

The site must then be made as free from sharp stones as possible. Carefully examine the base and sides and remove any stones which you think might pierce the liner. The excavation should also be free from small hollows. A hollow left under the skin of the liner, if walked on, could result in a tear, especially if the liner has little elasticity. The base (and sides if they are sloping) should then be given a 'blinding' of fine sand to a depth of about 7 cm.

To calculate the size of liner you require,

measure the depth of your pond, its length and its width. The length of liner required will be: twice the depth plus the length. Add to this figure about 60 cm to allow the liner to be secured under the paving slabs. Similarly, the width of the liner will be: twice the depth plus the width of the pond, plus 60 cm. In other words, a rectangular pond whose dimensions are 300 × 200 × 75 deep, would require a liner 510 × 410 cm. If the pond is an informal one of irregular depth and shape, then the calculations should be based on the maximum depth, length and width. If marginal shelves are incorporated in your design, then they must be taken into account when calculating the size of the liner. The method is the same as for an irregular pond: simply use a tape measure, and starting from one bank drape it across the floor of the site and up to the top of the far bank. Marginal shelves are used to support basket-grown aquatic plants which must be near the surface of the water. Make your shelves about 25 to 30 cm deep and about 30 cm

A Butyl rubber liner draped in the excavation. Filling the pond with water, prior to securing the liner, ensures a snug fit.

wide. Alternatively, the containers can be supported on concrete blocks placed in the pond after the liner has been laid. Make sure the concrete blocks are smooth, and lay additional pieces of PVC or thick polythene underneath them as added protection for the liner. This is a better procedure if the ground around your site is very crumbly and shelves can not be cut neatly.

If you are installing a non-stretchable liner, it will be necessary to smooth the liner around the banks by hand. First of all, lay the liner roughly in place. Then play a hose on the centre of the liner. As the water fills up, go round the pond straightening, overlapping and adjusting the liner as necessary. The object of the exercise is to get as smooth a finish as possible. Stretchable liners such as PVC and particularly Butyl rubber wrinkle much less and produce a much smoother finish. Spread the liner in the excavated site and hold in place with a few bricks or large stones around the perimeter. Apply water from the hose and as the pond fills up the elastic liner will mould itself, as it were, to the excavation. Little manipulation of the liner is required, except occasionally letting the

Overlapping of the liner can be completely avoided if one uses a three-dimensional liner, which is simply slotted into the 'trough'. Secure under the coping or glue to the walls.

PVC and Butyl rubber are available in certain widths and lengths, but manufacturers will join up sheets to provide a liner of any size that you require. In addition, some suppliers will weld Butyl sheets to form a three-dimensional liner, i.e. the joints are welded so as to provide sides and a base instead of just a plain welded sheet. A liner made in this way, be it a plain rectangle or any other formal shape, can be simply dropped into the excavation and there will be no wrinkling or overlapping whatsoever. When using a plain sheet, do not rely unduly on the elasticity of the material to obtain a smooth finish. Commonsense suggests that the less tension put on a liner the better. Above all make quite sure the liner is in contact at every point with the banks and base of the excavation, and that there is no gap where banks and base meet, which is a danger point. Once you are satisfied that the liner is in place properly, the perimeter can be cemented under the patio slabs.

liner slacken from under a brick or two, or conversely, pulling the liner up under others. However, in a pond of formal shape, such as a rectangle, a certain amount of overlapping at each corner is inevitable. If desired the overlapped sections or tucks can be glued to the sides. Use Bostik for PVC and a rubber glue for Butyl.

Liners have largely superseded concrete for the construction of ponds, for while the cost of liners and concrete is similar, the saving in labour is very considerable. In

Fig. 2. It is essential that the liner is touching the site at every point, as in the right-hand drawing. Securing the liner under the paving slabs before filling the pond at least half full with water may mean the liner is pulled away from the base and bank, as in the left-hand drawing.

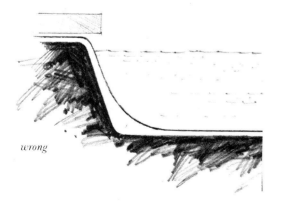

wrong

right

addition, liners can be repaired, even re-placed with comparative ease. Concrete, which is susceptible to cracking, especially under the pressure of ice, cannot be repaired with confidence. Relining a concrete pond involves breaking up the original concrete, a tiresome job, or concreting over the old concrete which means a smaller pond. (An easier solution is to lay a liner over the old concrete, having removed any sharp projections or loose pieces of concrete.) A concrete pond once made cannot be modified – the level of the banks must be got right first time – and the pond must be made to the highest standards. But there will always be people for whom the solidity of concrete, and the fact that it cannot be pierced or punctured, is sufficient justification for using the material.

To begin with, the excavation must be quite firm. If your excavation is in any way unstable, hard core (gravel, chippings, any kind of rubble that does not contain organic material) should be added to the base to a depth of about 100 mm and well compacted. Bear in mind that the excavated site must be larger than the finished pond by the thickness of the concrete. In the case of a pond sunk in a lawn, precise measurements might not be important. But if a pond is to be met by patio slabs around the perimeter, then the exact location and dimensions become critical.

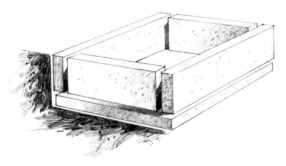

Fig. 3. To estimate the amount of concrete you require (so as to avoid overlapping), imagine that your pond will consist of these sections. The actual construction would not, of course, involve all these joints. All the sides are usually made in a single operation.

The problem of a leaking concrete pond is most easily solved by overlaying the concrete with a flexible liner, seen here by having the water level lowered. The pebbles around the bank are purely ornamental.

The concrete base of the pond should be at least 150 mm thick, and the sides preferably the same, certainly not less than 100 mm. This means that if your excavation measures 3.20 × 3.00 × 0.75 m deep, the internal measurements of the finished concrete pond will be 2.9 × 1.7 × 0.6 m deep.

To calculate the amount of concrete you require, first work out the area of the base and four sides. Then add these figures together and multiply by the thickness of the concrete. Remember to subtract the thickness of the base from the height of the walls, and the thickness of two walls from the length of the two opposing walls. This may seem very complicated, but in practice it is much less so. Using the above example of an excavation 3.20 × 2.00 × 0.75 m, the calculations are as follows. The depth of the pond will be 600 mm (i.e. 750 mm less 150 mm, the thickness of the concrete). Similarly, the thickness of two walls, 300 mm, must be subtracted from two opposing walls, 2.00 – 0.30 = 1.70 m.

base: 2 × 3.20 = 6.40 sq. metres
the two longer sides: 2(3.20 × 0.60) = 3.84 sq. metres

the two shorter sides: $2(1.7 \times 0.60) = 2.04$
sq. metres

The total area is, therefore, 12.28 sq. m.

Multiplying this figure by the thickness of concrete required provides the total amount of concrete required:

$12.28 \times 0.15 = 1.842$ cubic metres of concrete.

In round figures then, the pond requires 2 cubic metres of concrete. It is always advisable to round up your estimate to allow for wastage.

The concrete should consist of cement, sand and coarse aggregate in the ratio 1:2:3. The coarse aggregate can be either gravel or crushed stone varying in size from 5 mm to 20 mm. Make certain that your materials are quite free from any organic matter such as leaves. The amount of each material can be calculated as a proportion of 6, because the ratio 1:2:3 makes up a total of 6 parts. (See also Appendix III.) In 2 cubic metres of concrete:

the amount of cement will be $\frac{1}{6}$ of $2 = 0.33$ cubic metre

the amount of sand will be $\frac{2}{6}$ of $2 = 0.67$ cubic metre

the amount of aggregate will be $\frac{3}{6}$ of $2 = 1.00$ cubic metre

Building merchants do not normally provide exact amounts of sand and aggregate. They tend to estimate each order in relation to what their lorry holds, or some other rule of thumb. Measure out the proportions you require yourself, using a unit of measure such as a bucket or wheelbarrow. Sand and gravel can be bought already mixed. This is known as all-in aggregate. Make sure you specify the ratio you want. (See also Appendix III.) Add a waterproofer if you wish, but concrete that is properly mixed and compacted is impermeable on its own account.

First mix the materials dry. Begin by mixing the sand and the coarse aggregate, then add the cement. Dividing the mix into separate mounds and then uniting them into one is a good way of making sure the materials are properly interspersed. When all three are well mixed, make a depression in the middle of the heap and add water. Turn the mix over, working round it, heaping the dry material from the outside into the centre. Continue to add water until the *whole* heap is of the right consistency. Too much water reduces the strength of concrete. The right consistency has been achieved if you can slice the heap of concrete without the two sides fully uniting again. The mix should be firm and stiff, but also pliable. What you do not want is a mix with water running out of it. You might find it worthwhile to hire a small, portable cement mixer. The method of mixing differs slightly from mixing by hand. First add half the aggregate and a quantity of water, then add the sand. When they are mixed, add the cement followed by the rest of the aggregate. Add sufficient water to obtain the right consistency. Ready-mixed concrete offers a great saving in labour and effort where large ponds are concerned. The lorry must, of course, be able to get reasonably close to the site if not on to it. Ready-mixed concrete becomes economic when delivered in loads of about 3 cubic metres and upwards. Always specify the ratio of materials that you want.

In warm weather, concrete starts setting perceptibly in about twenty minutes. Continually turning over the mix will slow the process down. The more slowly the concrete dries out, the stronger it will be. For this reason, if the excavation is very dry and absorbent, it is worth lightly dowsing the base and sides with water. In hot weather, polythene or even wet newspaper should be placed over the newly laid concrete to retain moisture. Concrete continues to harden over a period of days and even weeks. Surprisingly, concrete hardens well under water. So once the initial hardening has taken place, fill up your pond with water. This can be done the day after the concrete has been laid. But on no account walk in the pond, or otherwise disturb it for at least three or four days. Making a concrete pond in frosty weather should be avoided. But if a *light* frost is expected during the night, lay a sheet of polythene over the pond. The polythene must be raised above the concrete, as it is the air trapped under the polythene that provides the protection.

The concrete will need to be reinforced. Ordinary chicken-wire, provided it is quite free from paint or leaves, does very well. If the wire is a little rusty that is no harm, provided it is still strong. For larger ponds, it is as well to use reinforcing rods about 10 mm in diameter, in addition to the chicken-wire. Rods of this thickness are quite strong enough for ponds, but they are relatively easy to bend to any required shape.

Let us say it is a small, formal pond that you are making. Then first lay in a layer of concrete over the entire base. On top of that put down the chicken-wire that you have already cut to shape. If the wire is not long enough and wide enough to run up the sides, then make sure it protrudes around the edge of the base. Having laid down the chicken-wire, add concrete to the base until you have a thickness of not less than 150 mm. This can be judged simply enough by a series of raised pegs set in the base. These must, of course, be removed before the concrete hardens and the holes they leave smoothed over. The concrete must be very firmly tamped down. No air pockets must be allowed to remain in or around the chicken-wire. Leave the concrete for a short time, then before it has quite set,

Fig. 4. Shuttering for a concrete pond.

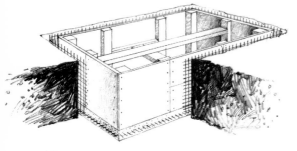

roughen up the perimeter with a knife or sharp stick, so that the base has a good 'key' for the sides. Finally smooth the base with a builder's float. When the concrete is hard, place in position the chicken-wire for the sides, attaching it to the wire protruding from the base. Then set up the shuttering. This can be made of timber, hardboard or any strong material. What is important is that it can be easily dismantled. You can rub a soapy cloth over the shuttering if you wish. This does help to prevent the concrete adhering to the shuttering. Above all, prevent soil from the surrounding banks falling on to the base. If soil gets into the joint between the base and the sides, the pond is very likely to leak. Concrete must then be worked between the shuttering and the banks. This can be quite awkward. The chicken-wire tends to slip down. The banks crumble. Always have the chicken-wire standing well proud of the shuttering. It can be held while the concrete is being forced into place and cut later. In a small pond, which one can stretch across or stand astride, the shuttering can often be put in place and the sides made immediately after the base has been laid, in a single operation.

In the case of informal ponds with sloping sides, the whole pond can often be made in a single operation and without shuttering. Take care that the sides are of uniform thickness, that they do not slump down and bulge where they meet the base. This will depend largely upon the consistency of your concrete. If you find that it is too soft, then leave it to stiffen. Shelves can be incorporated in the walls of an informal pond by cutting ledges in the site. But it is much simpler to make concrete shelves after the pond has been made.

New concrete secretes lime which can be fatal to plants and to fish. Either fill and empty the pond at least four if not six times over a period of several weeks (using a submersible electric pump is the easiest way of emptying the pond), or use a compound,

a

available from water garden centres, which is painted on to the concrete and seals in the lime. In time the sealer may wear off, but the process will be so gradual that no danger will arise. The pond is then ready for use. As you will appreciate, making a concrete pond involves a considerable amount of hard work. The result, however, should be very enduring.

These methods then are suitable for making a pond that is level with the patio. Raised ponds, however, require a slightly different approach, and that is the subject of the next chapter.

a) Using planks to barrow in the concrete avoids the risk of the banks collapsing; b) Finishing off the concrete with a builder's float; c) Making a marginal shelf; d) The finished pond.

c

b

d

3 The raised pond

A raised pond creates a welcome sense of solidity, brings the pond closer to view and is an attractive feature in its own right. It does not suit every situation, of course; its bulk can make a small patio look smaller. But if you decide upon making a raised pond, it is best to make it with a liner. I cannot see the point of taking the risk of concrete cracking. Unlike a pond level with the patio, a raised pond has nothing to counteract the pressure of water and the formation of ice can exert considerable pressure.

Normally, a raised pond made with a liner requires a double wall to provide sufficient strength. The length and width of the pond, assuming it to be a simple rectangle, should be multiples of the individual brick or block that you intend using. If the pond has different dimensions, then it may mean you have to keep cutting the brick to odd sizes. Not only is that an unnecessary chore, it is time-consuming and may affect the appearance of the wall. Let us say that you are using bricks 215 mm in length and you intend making the mortar joint between the bricks about 10 mm thick. Then to all intents and purposes your wall will be made up of 225 mm units. Make a rough estimate of the size of pond you want, say it is 3×1.8 metres. Then divide the length and the width of the pond by the length of one brick. i.e. $3000 \div 225 = 13 \, (13.3)$ and $1800 \div 225 = 8$. In other words 13 bricks are required for the length of the pond and 8 for the width. (In the case of the length the fraction is not significant because the mortar joint can be adjusted. In the case of a very small pond, however, the dimensions of the pond itself might have to be adjusted.) To calculate the number of bricks required for a single course the whole way round the pond, the bricks for the length and width of the pond are simply doubled, i.e. $2(13 + 8) = 42$ bricks. The number of courses required can be calculated by dividing the height of the pond by the height of a single brick. For example, let us say the pond is to be 600 mm high and the brick is 75 mm high (65 mm plus 10 mm joint), then $600 \div 75 = 8$ courses. (Remember that the liner is usually tucked in under the top course of bricks, so the depth of the pond will be less than the height of the surrounding wall by one course. It is normal practice to lay the final course of brick, the coping, on edge as opposed to 'on the 'flat' (see page 22). This makes a slight difference to the overall height but greatly improves the appearance of the wall.) The total number of bricks required for the pond is simply the number of bricks required for a single course multiplied by the number of courses, i.e. $42 \times 8 = 336$ bricks. If, however, you intend using 'on edge' coping, then the coping course will require almost 3 times as many bricks as a stretcher course, i.e. $3 \times 42 = 126$. The total number of bricks would then be $42 \times 7 + 126 = 420$. The inner wall can be calculated in the same way. It is more economical here if concrete blocks are used.

A raised brick pond finished with coping laid on edge.

They will not, of course, be seen.

When ordering your building materials it is as well to slightly overestimate the number of bricks and blocks you require to allow for breakage. The inner wall will almost certainly require the cutting of some of the blocks and this may involve additional wastage. There are two methods of cutting bricks or blocks. The cleaner and quicker method is by means of a hydraulic stone cutter, a machine not unlike a guillotine. The brick is placed on a cutting block and the cutter is then operated by a handle. You simply slice through the brick. Hydraulic stone cutters are not always easy to obtain on hire and the cost is only justified if you have a very large number of bricks – or paving slabs – to cut. The usual method is by means of a club hammer and bolster chisel. First chip

away a line the whole way round the brick or block at the point where you want it to break. Then place the bolster in the indentation and give it a sharp – unhesitating – tap with the hammer. The brick should then break cleanly along the indentation. A little practice may be required to obtain clean cuts, but there is no real difficulty involved.

Hydraulic stone-splitter.

Cutting a brick with a club hammer and bolster chisel.

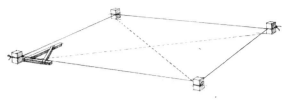

Fig. 5. *Marking out an area using pegs and a builder's line. Make sure the diagonals are of equal length. Check corners with a 3:4:5 triangle (see page 56).*

Having calculated the dimensions of your pond, the next step is to mark out the perimeter with a builder's line and pegs. Check that the corners are right-angles by measuring the diagonals. If the diagonals are of equal length then the four corners must be right-angles. Also make quite certain that the pond is parallel with adjacent walls. The width of the foundation must be greater than the width of the walls. There are two reasons for this. It will provide you with a certain amount of latitude as regards the precise positioning of the pond; but much more important, if the pond walls are to be perfectly stable, the foundation must be of a greater width. The normal practice is for the foundation to be dug down below the level of the top soil and the top of the concrete is kept well below surface level. (To determine the

depth and width of foundation you require, refer to Appendix III.) Use pegs to make certain the foundation will be level the whole way round. Simply drive the pegs into the trench at intervals and level them with a straight board and spirit level. The pegs can be left in the trench until it has been filled with concrete and then removed before the concrete has set.

The amount of concrete required for the foundation can be calculated in the same way as for concrete ponds (see page 16). Less cement, however, is needed: 1 part cement, $2\frac{1}{2}$ parts of sand and 5 parts of coarse aggregate is satisfactory. Mix the materials dry and add no more water than is required to obtain a heavy, thick consistency. Place the concrete in the trench, compact it well and level off.

The techniques for building the walls of a raised pond are similar to those required for building a wall round a patio. (For a full discussion see Chapter 6.) The only significant difference is that your pond will usually involve building a double leaf wall, whereas a patio wall may be single or double leaf. When building a pond, it is easier to complete the inner leaf first. But set out at least a single course of the outer wall first. It is the position of the outer wall which is critical.

Fig. 6. *Levelling a foundation trench with pegs, straight edge and a builder's level.*

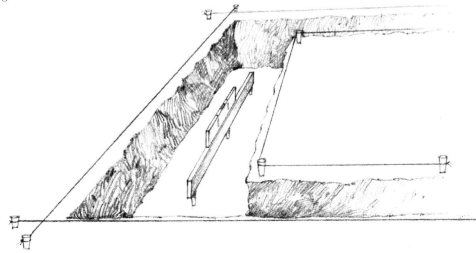

Laying out the first course of bricks dry, a most important procedure.

Construction of a raised pond involves a double leaf wall. A saving in time and cost can be made by using concrete blocks for the inner leaf.

Lay the complete course dry first of all. Make sure the corners are correctly positioned, then cement them in place. The rest of the course can then be laid. Both bricks and blocks must be staggered. That is to say the joints in each course should coincide with the middle of each brick in the course above and below. On no account should joints be lined up one above the other. If this were done the strength of the wall would be drastically impaired. The staggering of courses is easily achieved by the arrangement of the corner bricks.

The distance at which the two leaves or walls stand is important if you intend using brick as a coping. Coping is normally placed at right angles across the wall. So the combined width of the two leaves should exactly equal the length of one brick

If you are building a double leaf wall, the leaves should be united to combine their strength. This can be done by using what are known as ties or butterflies. These are lengths of wire or plastic bent or shaped in a figure-of-eight or similar pattern. Flat pieces of metal with twisted ends to provide anchor-

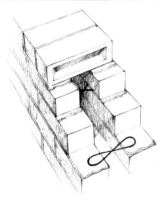

Fig. 7. Butterflies can be used to unite a double leaf wall. For clarity, the distance between the two leaves is exaggerated in the illustration.

24

hardly noticeable, but with small ponds the brickwork may appear as very rough and ready. A possible solution is to lay the bricks in alternate stretcher and header courses, or in header courses entirely. Care must still be taken to ensure that the bricks are evenly staggered. The joints at the wall face will be somewhat enlarged but this need not matter

age are also used. The ties are inserted in each course at intervals of about every three or four bricks. They should be staggered so that no two ties are directly above one another. The protruding end of the tie is then inserted in the second leaf as it is being built. Alternatively, bed in mortar between the two walls during construction. Where hard winters are a problem this method will provide the walls with immense strength. One point to remember, however, is to remove, first of all, the loose mortar which will have fallen between the two leaves. Otherwise the fresh mortar packed between the two leaves will have little chance of bonding with the foundation.

There is one situation where a double leaf wall, consisting of two quite separate leaves, is impractical. That is where the pond is circular and made on a small radius. The problem then arises that the bricks do not align properly when staggered. The problem is highlighted in the figure and you can see how bricks, unless they have a curved face, tend to protrude in alternate courses. In the case of large, sweeping ponds this may be

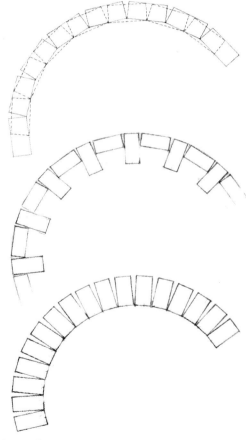

Fig. 8. The problem of how bricks protrude in alternate courses in a curved wall is highlighted in the top diagram. Two ways of minimising the problem are illustrated beneath.

A circular pond with a well-made raised kerbing.

too much. A former made of light plywood can be used as an aid to maintain an even curve. The brick courses are built up against the former. However, it must be said that building a circular pond requires considerable skill.

The last course of bricks or the coping should not be put on until the liner has been put in place. Fill the pond at least half full with water so that a snug fit is obtained for the liner. Do not stretch the liner unduly and above all make sure it is in contact with the brickwork at all points. As illustrated on page 15 it is easy to leave a gap at the point where the base meets the wall. This is why it is worth putting water in the pond before securing the coping, as the water will ensure

that the liner is completely in contact with the structure. It should not be necessary to plaster the interior of the walls but do make sure there are no sharp pieces of mortar protruding from the joints. Knock these off, sweep up all debris from the base and lay in a few centimetres of sand before putting in the liner. Then aim for a smooth but not unnecessarily taut fitting. Cut the liner carefully so that its perimeter extends about half-way over the top of the brick. The coping can then be cemented in place. If for any reason you want the water level to be at the same height as the surrounding wall, then the liner must be glued in position and a suitable sealing compound run round the top of the liner. This method can also be used if

Raised ponds bring all the inhabitants of the pond, fish and plants, closer to view. The elderly and the disabled will find a raised pond easier to maintain, and a broad, flat coping, be it of concrete or brick, is useful for sitting upon.

you wish to replace a liner without removing the coping. However, securing the liner under the coping is preferable.

Apart from brick, coping of various shapes and sizes can be bought. Flat coping is best if you want to sit at the edge of the pond and enjoy the plants and underwater world of fish and insect life. You can also make your own coping by using wooden moulds. The concrete should be in the ratio 1 part cement, 2 of sand and 3 of coarse aggregate (or use more sand and less aggregate if you want a smoother finish). Making your own coping is troublesome as opposed to buying it. However, there are situations where coping of a particular width or size is not available, so it is worth mentioning the option of making it at home. Coping so made should not be less than 75 mm thick and lengths above 1 metre (when about 200 mm wide) become vulnerable to cracking when laid without reinforcement.

These then are the most common techniques used for pond building. They are the most common because they are the most trouble-free. We can now turn to the subject of ornamental fountains and waterfalls.

4 Ornamental fountains and waterfalls

Water has a dual personality. Placid, unstirred by any breeze, mirroring in every detail surrounding plants and a cloudless sky; supporting motionless leaves and flowers of water-lilies: that is one side of the personality. The other side is utterly different. Tumbling, tinkling, bubbling cascades, or foam journeying over rock, brick or other impediment; or rising from a fountain, dividing into tiny drops to fall in iridescent circles. That side of water is all animation. The two sides are by no means incompatible. A fountain or waterfall can be combined with a pond, without the fountain being run continuously. Or in the case of a medium or large size pond, one end can contain the animation of the waterfall or fountain, while the other can remain relatively undisturbed.

But there is another alternative altogether. One which should appeal to the patio owner for whom water and more specifically fountains are the thing, rather than water-lilies and plants. The smallest of patios can accommodate a small fountain. It can set off the entire patio, and unlike plants a fountain does not, of course, depend upon an adequate amount of sunlight. Moreover, a fountain ornament has a particular value for those who use their patio for entertainment. Curious as it may seem, people tend to be self-conscious in forming themselves into groups when confronted with a bare patio space; but where there is an obvious focal point, a central feature, people do form groups more

naturally. There is another consideration. The danger of ponds (of whatever depth) where young children are concerned, has already been mentioned. An ornamental fountain or statue which has a high shallow bowl and a reservoir concealed in the stem offers a safer alternative. If the fountain does not have a reservoir, one can be made by any of the methods described for making a pond and concealed under the fountain. Or because it will be concealed, use a galvanised tank. What is important is that the tank is narrow enough for it to be safely covered by your paving slabs. Water from the fountain

A fountain with a concealed – and safe – reservoir. Note that some water is getting on the paving, an indication that the area enclosed by the kerbing should be larger. The pebbles are laid over a grid which sits on top of the reservoir.

29

or statue should be arranged so that it flows down through a small grating in the patio. This may require an edging of brick, if the flow of water is considerable, so that the patio is kept dry.

In many countries where water is a comparatively scarce commodity involving restrictions during the summer months, people are, understandably, discouraged from using water as an ornamental feature. Why build a pond if it is likely to dry out for months at a time? The concealed reservoir is an excellent way of reducing evaporation to a minimum. Almost all the evaporation will be limited to the water as it circulates on the statue or ornament, and this should amount to very little.

Fountains were once operated by the artesian principle and occasionally one still sees them, mainly in the grandiose gardens of earlier days, such as those at Villa d'Este outside Rome. Nowadays garden fountains and waterfalls are powered by an electric pump which continually re-cycles the same water. Whether you intend having a waterfall or fountain, or indeed both, there are two basic types of pump from which to choose, the submersible pump and the land or surface pump.

The most commonly used pump is the submersible one. It is easier to install. One simply places the pump on the bottom of the pond or reservoir and the electric cable from it is connected to an electric point at a safe distance from the water. (All electrical connections should be carried out by a qualified electrician.) Some of the less powerful submersible pumps run at less than the full voltage rating and so require a transformer which is connected up between the mains and the pump.

In addition to a pump all you need to make a display fountain is a length of plastic tubing of the right diameter and a nozzle or jet to provide the kind of fountain you want. The range of nozzles and jets is now vast. You can even buy jets which continually change the

Fig. 9. A fountain fed not by a pump but by gravity: the artesian principle.

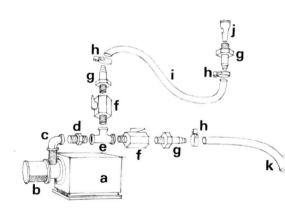

Fig. 10. Submersible pump **a** with fittings: **b** strainer, usually supplied with pump, **c** 'L' bend with male and female thread screws, **d** hexagonal nipple, with two male threads, **e** Pitcher Tee or 'T' piece, **f** gate-valve, **g** hose union, **h** jubilee clip, **i** outlet pipe for fountain, **j** fountain jet, **k** outlet pipe for waterfall.

If the outlet pipe from the pump is inserted in another pool (at the top of a waterfall for example), and if you want to ensure that the top pool does not empty into the lower one through the pipe, you should fit the outlet pipe with a non-return valve.

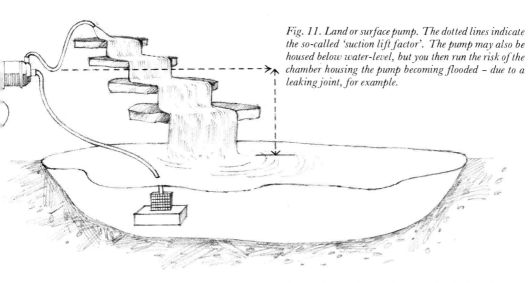

Fig. 11. Land or surface pump. The dotted lines indicate the so-called 'suction lift factor'. The pump may also be housed below water-level, but you then run the risk of the chamber housing the pump becoming flooded – due to a leaking joint, for example.

pattern of the spray. A valve with which to regulate the flow of water is a useful extra. It should be connected at a convenient point in the plastic tubing. You need nothing else except jubilee clips with which to connect up the tubing. If you want to have a simple fountain in a pond, then the nozzle or jet should stand just clear of the surface of the water. If necessary raise the pump up on blocks so that the plastic tubing is not unduly long. It may tend to sag. If you are using a fountain ornament or statue, the plastic tubing is simply connected up to a pipe which emerges discreetly from the ornament at some point; or the plastic tubing is threaded through the ornament as far as the point of exit. If you are not using a nozzle or jet, the plastic tubing must be cut straight across. Otherwise the water may tend to come out at an odd angle. One point often overlooked (even by those who ought to know better) is that the spray of the fountain must not go over the edge of the pond. If it does, you will find the level of the pond declining with surprising speed. What might seem like an insignificant spattering on the edge of the patio amounts over a period of hours to more water than one might imagine. As a rule the dimensions of the pond should not be less than twice the height of the

fountain jet. If you have a single jet of water rising, say, 75 cm, then the width of the pool should not be less than 1.5 metres, and even then anything stronger than a light breeze may well take spray on to the patio. If the fountain is not a single spout of water but a circular spray, then add at least the radius of the circle to the previous calculation.

If you should choose a land or surface pump in preference to a submersible one, it must be installed in a weatherproof container adjacent to the pond. The container can be made of concrete blocks, for example, and conveniently covered by a paving slab. On no account should the container be subject to flooding. Not only might that ruin the pump, it could be highly dangerous. Air must be able to circulate freely round the pump so that it does not overheat and so that any dampness can escape. An intake pipe is then brought from the pump to the pond and an outlet pipe directed to the top of the waterfall or to the fountain ornament as the case may be.

The pump must be primed with water before it will operate. The easiest way of doing this is to insert a hose pipe into the outlet pipe, just a few centimetres is sufficient. Then allow water to run through the system. You will see bubbles rising from the pond as air is expelled from the pump and pipes. After a minute or two, when the bubbles have ceased, start the pump and withdraw the hosepipe. The pump should then operate fully. If not, repeat the procedure allowing the pump a little longer to become primed. If the pump is situated below the surface level of the water in the pond, then it will retain its prime even when switched off. If it is above the water level the prime must be maintained by using a foot-valve, which is usually incorporated in a strainer. A strainer is an essential piece of equipment as it will prevent debris from entering the pump and possibly damaging it. If you are including a regulator valve in the system make sure it is connected to the outlet pipe. On no account should the intake pipe be interfered with in any way. The pump may suffer damage if the intake pipe is restricted. If, for any reason, you have to

A fish hide supporting a submersible pump. Always keep your pump off the base of the pond where it may become clogged with debris.

install your pump at some height above the pond, check what is known as the suction lift factor. This is the maximum height at which a given pump can raise water. It will be stated on the manufacturer's instructions. Rarely is this a problem, however, as the suction lift factor is not likely to be less than 1.5 metres.

When should one choose a surface pump and when a submersible one? A surface pump is called for only if a gigantic water display is required – the kind of display that one associates with great houses and public parks rather than back gardens. At that level of performance a land pump may be more economical to buy. Even then one has to take into account the additional cost of housing and plumbing. Certainly for convenience and trouble-free running a submersible pump is the better choice. If you raise the pump up above the floor of the pond on blocks or a fish hide, that will help to keep it free from debris. A submersible pump is never likely to run dry; but a land pump can easily do so and will burn out as a result. On the other hand, if a land pump is housed below water level, some precaution must be taken to prevent the container or chamber in which it is housed from flooding when the intake pipe is disconnected. (Raising the end of the outlet pipe above water level is usually the easiest way.) This point might not seem significant when described. Experience suggests otherwise. Plumbing a land pump in a confined space can be very awkward.

The performance of pumps is usually measured as output in relation to a given 'head', that is the vertical height of the output pipe above water-level. The greater the head the smaller will be the output. Generally speaking, the performance of surface pumps is affected less by an increase in head than are submersible pumps. The length and bore of the outlet pipe may also affect the performance to a small extent due

A patio pond having a fountain ornament and a glass-fibre waterfall (or cascade) powered by a single submersible pump with a Pitcher Tee or 'T' piece (see page 30).

to friction, more so if the pipe contains a number of twists and bends. Again the effect is usually less on surface pumps. Manufacturers normally provide performance tables, which are sometimes pitched a little optimistically; but comparisons can be usefully made.

The question then is how powerful should a pump be for a given situation? The most practical, if hardly the most helpful, advice is that there is nothing better than seeing how a specific pump performs with a particular jet or ornament. However, the field can be narrowed to some extent. The smallest pumps, for garden use, have a maximum output of between 15 and 20 litres a minute (200–265 gallons per hour). Such a pump would provide a tiny fountain no more than a few centimetres high, or a very light, tinkling flow of water on an ornament. If you have a

A small patio pond combined with modern sculptural pre-cast concrete units, which are in fact a series of fountains.

very small pond or statue fountain, then a pump with that capacity would be sufficient. However, the average suburban patio pond is likely to require a performance more in the region of 25 to 35 lpm (333–466 gph). Remember that the kind of nozzle, if you are using one, will be a factor in the pressure the pump must overcome. Pumps in this range are very cheap to run. They consume much the same amount of electricity as an ordinary light bulb. To produce a cascade of water, one would need a pump of considerably greater power. Again the size, shape and height of the cascade are important. But as a rough guide it can be said that a vigorous cascade would need an output of perhaps 40 to 60 lpm (533–800 gph), but of course much more powerful submersible and land pumps are available.

Most patios and patio ponds are formal in design. If a waterfall is to be included in the design then it should be in keeping with everything else. A natural waterfall in a formal setting is quite out of place. Besides, the scope for design of formal waterfalls is limitless. Basically, what one needs are a series of receptacles, one arranged above the other, so that each one catches the water as it overflows from the receptacle above. Concrete is a suitable material with which to make such receptacles. Make a series of wooden moulds consisting of two frames, one fitting inside the other. The idea is to make a series of concrete lidless boxes which will hold water. The walls need to be about 10 mm thick and preferably reinforced with chicken wire. However, it must be said that the danger of concrete cracking in winter is considerable, so that this method is best suited to areas with frost-free winters. Otherwise, drain the receptacles in winter. An essential feature for each receptacle is an adequate 'lip', otherwise the water will not so much pour from the receptacle as dribble down the side. The lip can be made from lead, aluminium or even a section cut from plastic guttering. If the pond is set against a

A traditional pre-cast concrete fountain made up of five separate units.

wall, the receptacles can be mounted on the wall by means of steel rods. Alternatively, they can be set in a column situated in the centre of the pond. Either way the receptacles will need suitable holes for securing to the rods. Either place small pieces of dowelling in the moulds, or drill the required holes after the concrete has fully set. A great deal of trial and error will be required before the receptacles are aligned to produce a waterfall that is satisfying. You will find at first that the water streams down the side of one receptacle, spatters over another and generally does not fall directly from one receptacle to the next. One has no choice but to experiment until the required effect is achieved. Usually it is an advantage to have the receptacle tilting forward slightly. The water pours better when the lip (or spout) is inclined at an angle. Care must be taken to ensure that no water splashes on to an adjacent wall or on to the patio, if the water level in the pond is to remain constant. The rods can be set in mortar, but if a great deal of

experimenting with the receptacles is found necessary, use putty instead.

There is another kind of formal waterfall which has been introduced in recent years, in which the idea of receptacles which hold water is discarded altogether. Instead a series of fins are inserted in the wall or column to deflect the water as it falls. Not only can this, if carefully done, produce wonderfully varied effects, but the sound of tinkling water broken at many points in this way has a peculiar fascination of its own. Small sheets of aluminium or non-rust metal should be soldered or welded on to thin rods, so that they look rather like miniature flags. The fins are then arranged in the same way as receptacles.

A problem when using a wall for a waterfall is how to conceal the outlet pipe coming from the pump. Ideally, if it is a double wall, the pipe can be placed between the two courses as the wall is being built. If the wall is already standing, but is not too

Fig. 12. A waterfall made with a series of 'fins' or 'flags'.

A fountain mask framed in brickwork. The outlet pipe of the pump is concealed in the wall.

high, it is sometimes possible to remove the coping and by some deft manoeuvring, thread the pipe through. Otherwise it means removing bricks or making a channel through a block wall with hammer and chisel and re-plastering afterwards. Either method will leave obvious tell-tale marks. New bricks never look the same as old, new plaster never merges with old. This may be sufficient reason for choosing an alternative water feature.

There are two situations where a natural waterfall might be suitable for a patio pond: in the rare case where an irregular-shaped pond is bordered by a rockery, or when a water feature is made the subject of a raised bed (the walls of the bed then frame the natural feature in the way that a picture might be framed). Cascades can be made from a series of irregular concrete 'bowls', but it is a difficult and time-consuming

Below: an informal pond with well-constructed stone work. Right: an outstanding example of a perfectly natural-looking waterfall made with a flexible liner.

A waterfall made with a concrete 'bowl' or cascade.

method. They need not be made *in situ.*
Indeed there is an advantage in making them
off site, provided they are small enough to be
lifted afterwards. Make a depression in soft
ground to act as a mould. Line with
polythene or newspaper. Then proceed to
lay in your concrete, with chicken-wire
reinforcement. Do not make the bowl too
shallow, otherwise it may dry out; 150 mm is
not too deep. Make a lip by embedding a
piece of slate or flat stone. The positioning of
the lip is important. Remember that water
builds up to a perceptible height in a cascade
before it flows out. So make sure the lip is
several centimetres below the surrounding
edge of the cascade. Natural cascades are
only likely to be installed in a rockery. Once
they are quite set, they can be placed in
depressions made in the soil. You might ask,
why not make the cascades *in situ*? Simply
because it is almost impossible to get their
positioning right without adjusting them
while the waterfall is running. Each cascade
must be situated well under the one above,

otherwise water is bound to get on to the
surrounding soil. Do not attempt to bring the
outlet pipe through the side of the top
cascade. Water will seep out between the
pipe and the concrete. The pipe must be
brought over the top of the cascade. Conceal
it with a plant. If you want to disguise the
concrete cascades, bed in rocks around the
edge (using mortar as sparingly as you can).
Do not bed rocks into the cascades while
making them, as that may impair the
strength of the concrete.

To make a water course, in which the
water travels over an irregular surface (but
does not descend through the air necessarily), one is better using liner material as
the foundation. Concrete can be used, being
laid *in situ*, but it has the distinct disadvantage of being inflexible. Once laid it cannot
be modified. A liner can be laid as a series of
overlapping sections (see fig. 13) if a single
sheet of the required length is not available.
A liner does allow experimenting, which is
almost essential if you have never previously

*Fig. 13. Making a liner waterfall. The liner must be
pulled well up the banks and then concealed and held in
place by rocks and stones lightly set in mortar.*

A pre-fabricated plastic cascade.

lights float if not anchored underwater by means of bricks placed over their cables. One of the finest effects that can be achieved with a patio pond is to have underwater lights positioned beneath and slightly behind a fountain spray. In that position the lights catch the sparkle and iridescence of the spray. On balmy, dark nights, with the aroma of the barbecue wafting across the patio, and underwater lighting playing on a fountain, the effect can be magical.

We now have covered the construction of ponds and water features. It is now time to consider the laying of the patio.

The effect of underwater lights can be most dramatic.

tried making a water course. Butyl rubber is the most suitable material, PVC being rather too easily damaged. If you are going to conceal the concrete or liner under rocks, make allowance for their size when deciding on the width of the water course. Excavate the soil to the shape you want and then lay down the liner. Allow yourself plenty of surplus liner so that folds and tucks can be incorporated as required. Glass-fibre and plastic cascades are available commercially. They do not, however, weather satisfactorily and tend to retain an artificial appearance. Lead sheeting has also been used successfully to make water courses. It is malleable, but once you have bent lead in one direction it tends to break if bent back again. Considerable time and skill is required to get the water to run along the course exactly as you want. Small rocks, representing boulders, can divert or divide the water as it tumbles down over nooks and crannies. The result can be very effective, but do make sure water is not lost by running over the side of the liner or foundation.

Finally, mention should be made of underwater lighting. Such lights are simply submerged in the pond at strategic points and directed at any special feature such as a fountain or wall mask. Some submersible

5 Laying the patio

If one were asked to say what constitutes the well laid patio, one would have to include at least five criteria in the answer. First of all the paving slabs should all be laid so that none stands proud of the one next to it. If one does, sooner or later someone will trip on it. Secondly, the patio should slant, however imperceptibly, away from the house so that the rain water is carried away. Thirdly, the patio should not collect huge pools of water. If the materials used and the laying technique employed make the surface impervious, then a gully trap would need to be put in with a soakaway. Fourthly, the patio should be laid below the damp course of the house to be quite certain that it will not create rising damp; and fifthly, the patio should not be subject to subsidence or the settling of what lies beneath it. If you are new to patio laying, you may have observed in magazines and the like, photographs of well dressed men (or women) with not a hair out of place, putting down a paving slab with what appears to be effortless ease. It is not quite like that. For the newcomer the strain on the back is considerable, even with small slabs. Remember the often repeated advice: lift by bending the knees, take the load with the legs, not the back. The hands can take quite rough treatment too. Use a pair of

A well-made, mature patio pond.

41

gloves if you do not find them too clumsy. To watch an experienced builder laying a patio (especially after one has laid a patio oneself) is to admire the way in which he can measure the right amount of foundation needed for each slab, how he taps it into place, neither too vigorously nor too softly, so that it ends absolutely level with its companion. Like most things, there is a knack to patio laying. The newcomer can do it successfully but progress will be slow.

The first thing to do is mark out the area for the patio. If the area is not already defined by existing boundary walls, try, if at all possible, to make the dimensions of the patio divisible by the paving elements to be used. This means, of course, choosing the paving slabs before deciding on the precise size of the patio. But if that means avoiding the tiresome and time-consuming task of cutting large numbers of slabs to fit the available space, then it is worthwhile. Similar consideration should be given to the exact dimensions and position of the pond. Even when cutting cannot be avoided altogether, a little forethought can often minimise it. Imagine, for example, that you want your patio to be about 12 m in length and you intend using paving slabs 600 mm square. Let us say too that you will leave an open joint of 5 mm between each slab. This should be added to the dimensions of the slab, so that the effective space required for each slab will be 605 mm square. If you divide 12 m by 605 mm you get 19.8 metres, which is the number of slabs required to run the length of the patio. But you can avoid the fraction by either making the length of the patio 12.10 m (20 × 605) or 11.50 m (19 × 605). In the same way try to round up or down the dimensions of the pond so that the paving slabs just overhang the banks by 25 mm, or thereabouts. If the area for the patio is already defined by boundary walls, then simply determine the number of slabs you need. This is done by dividing the length and width of the area by the length and width of a single

slab, and then multiplying these two figures together.

There is another point that needs considering before work begins. If your patio area is surrounded by walls, check to see that they are parallel. A surprising number of walls are not parallel; and adjacent walls, you may find, are not at perfect right-angles. If this proves the case there is nothing for it but to slice off ever larger sections from the slabs as you proceed along one wall. Choose the wall which is least exposed to view. If a wall is not perfectly straight, then either leave a gap between the patio slab and the wall equal to the depth of the 'wind' or curve, or cut slabs to accommodate the wind, and that is a tedious business.

When you come to lay your slabs a certain number are liable to get cracked or broken. Even the most experienced will lose a number. So add at least 5 per cent to your estimate.

The next stage is to level the entire area with a fall away from the house. The fall can be very slight, indeed the slightest gradient will be sufficient, i.e. 1:60. Water will be certain to follow the fall, and the patio will look far more satisfactory (especially if built against a brick wall with strong horizontal lines) if the gradient is not obvious to the eye. Level the entire area with a series of pegs, a straight edge and a level. To obtain a consistent fall, make a mark very slightly to one side of the bubble marks on your level. It must be very close to the existing mark, or you will end up with a fall that is far too steep. Begin with a datum peg close to the house and, working from that point, drive further pegs into the ground, levelling the area as you go. When taking readings parallel with the house, the normal markings on the level are, of course, used. Sometimes it is desirable to have a fall in more than one direction. In the photograph on pages 48–9, a feature has been made of a circle of bricks with a gully trap right in the centre. In this instance one would need, say, four datum pegs at the four

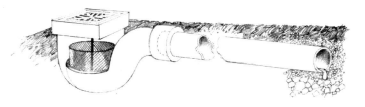

Fig. 14. A gully-trap containing a basket in which debris may be collected and easily removed. A grid at the top of the trap is essential whether there is a basket fitted or not.

corners of the patio and all exactly level. One would then work inwards to the centre point.

Once the area is quite level, tamp it down or use a roller to make firm. If you intend using the patio for foot traffic only, no further preparation should be necessary. The addition of hardcore, of small crushed stones, gravel or indeed any non-organic material, followed by a 'blinding' of sand, to a total depth of about 100 mm, need only be bedded in if the sub-soil is unstable.

There are basically four methods of laying paving elements. Some methods are more suitable than others, depending upon the type of paving. Concrete slabs can be laid in all four ways. Given a very firm surface, they can even be laid with no bedding material at all. This, however, leaves the slabs vulnerable to shifting, and the normal practice is to use a bedding material. You might choose to simply bed down the slabs on fine sand; a depth of 30 to 50 mm is quite adequate. Begin at one corner by the house (or the highest point of the patio), put down a convenient amount of sand and lay the first slab, bedding

it down so that it does not rock and at the same time has the requisite gradient. You can then proceed to lay another slab beside it, tapping it gently into place using a rubber-headed hammer, or an ordinary household hammer and a wooden block, or even a wooden mallet. As further slabs are laid, use the level and the straight edge, which should be long enough to extend over at least three slabs (see fig. 15). If you find that a slab remains too high after gentle tapping, or if it is too low, then there is nothing for it but to remove the slab and adjust the amount of sand beneath it.

Another way of levelling the slabs is by the use of a builder's line. Put down two slabs at

Fig. 15. Laying slabs on sand using a long straight edge to level them.

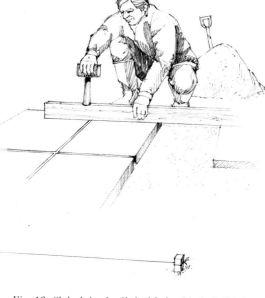

Fig. 16. Slabs being levelled with the aid of a builder's line.

Fig. 17. Using a series of pegs helps to ensure joints of uniform width.

either end of the patio, calculating the fall by means of the level and straight edge (using a series of pegs in the intervening space if necessary). The line is then stretched from the edge of one slab to the other, and can then be used as a guide while laying the intervening slabs.

If you are laying the slabs with open joints, as opposed to close joints, you may find a series of wooden pegs (about 10 to 15 mm square) inserted between the slabs will help to keep the joints of uniform width. The pegs can be removed as you proceed. It is a help, of course, if you have someone shovelling sand as you lay the slabs. Concrete slabs 600 mm square and 50 mm thick can be handled by one person. But slabs 600 × 900 mm are extremely heavy and require four hands to lay in place. If your patio is not bounded by walls on all sides, it will be necessary to prevent the sand from being washed out. When using concrete slabs it should be sufficient to simply bed down the perimeter slabs with mortar consisting of 1 part of cement to 3 of sand. If the patio borders on a lawn, make sure the slabs are a few centimetres lower than the lawn. This will make the grass easier to cut.

The second method of laying slabs is identical to the first, except that the bedding consists of dry mortar made up of 1 part cement to 3 of sand instead of pure sand. This should provide a firmer foundation. It will not harden fully until the patio is exposed to rain, and even then you may expect the hardening process to take perhaps several weeks. In the case of heavy concrete slabs this does not mean the patio should not be used at all, but heavy loads and, in particular, sudden vibrations should be avoided.

In the third method, the mortar is mixed with water to obtain a fairly stiff mix. The heavier the paving slab the stiffer should be the mix. Mix only a small amount of mortar at a time, especially during hot weather; otherwise it will become unworkable before it has all been laid. Continually adding water only reduces its strength. The advantage of using wet as opposed to dry mortar lies in the fact that wet mortar produces a better bond

Laying natural dressed stone on dry mortar. (For heavy traffic a concrete foundation would provide a firmer support and the slabs would be less vulnerable to cracking.)

with the paving slab. The disadvantage, apart from the additional labour involved, is that wet mortar is bound to get on your hands or gloves, and from there on to the upper surface of the slab. Mortar stains very readily and must be washed off before it dries out.

A fourth method is known as 'spot bedding'. Mortar is made up in the normal way but instead of spreading it under the entire paving slab, dollops of mortar are positioned on the ground where the four corners of the slab will lie. In the case of large slabs a fifth dollop should be placed in the middle. Upon these dollops the slab is placed and then tapped or squeezed down to make it level. There is an obvious saving in labour and materials in using this method. It is quite satisfactory for walking upon, but the slabs are rather more vulnerable to cracking and displacement if you have to continually drag a heavy lawnmower over them. Several days should elapse before you use a patio made in this way.

Fig. 18. Spot bedding with wet mortar.

The joints should then be grouted. If a wet mix is used, the mortar should be worked between the joints using a builder's trowel. As you work along keep wiping the paving slabs with a wet cloth or sponge to prevent staining. The use of a plywood template with a slot cut in it can be helpful. Finish the joints by smoothing with a piece of rubber tubing or bent pipe, so that the joint is slightly lower than the surface of the slabs. A more popular method of grouting is the dry mortar one, though it does not provide quite the same adhesion as the wet mortar method. Dry mortar is simply swept into the joints with a brush. The mortar is then wetted by means of a watering can with a fine rose. Care has to be taken to ensure that the mortar is not forced

out of the joints. Sand can also be used for the joints, or even soil if you intend growing prostrate plants between the paving slabs. While neither sand nor soil will bind the slabs as mortar will, they do have the advantage of allowing rain to soak through more quickly. Where heavy concrete slabs are concerned, they should remain perfectly stable irrespective of the joint filler. You might choose close joints instead of open ones, which do not require grouting at all. As against that, weeds will appear between the slabs no matter how closely they are placed together; and weeding is more difficult to carry out when the slabs are close jointed.

There are three ways in which paving slabs can be cut. The cheapest method is with a bolster chisel and lump hammer. The method is the same as for bricks. The slab is marked with chalk or scored with the bolster chisel. Using the hammer and chisel a groove is then made along the line. Place the chisel in the centre of the groove and give it a deft blow with the hammer. The slab should then break cleanly into two pieces. Working on a bed of sand makes the slab less likely to crack prematurely or in the wrong place. Alternatively, you can make the initial groove with a rotary disc cutter. These are easily

Scoring a slab with a rotary disc cutter.   45

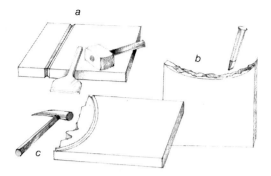

Fig. 19. Implements and their use: a) a slab scored with a hammer and chisel; b) a curve which has been chipped away with a cold chisel, and c) a builder's hammer.

hired and speed up the operation considerably; and with experience you should be able to make a clean break having cut a groove on only one side. Be sure to get the correct type of disc for the material you intend cutting. Ear muffs are worth having as protection against the noise of the cutter. Some manufacturers also recommend the use of protective goggles. If you have a great deal of cutting to do the fastest and cleanest cuts are obtained with a hydraulic stone splitter, but these are less easy to hire. Also, a stone splitter can not negotiate curves. If the curve is broad you can use a rotary disc cutter; otherwise use the chisel and hammer.

It is important how you measure up an area which requires less than a whole slab. Supposing, for example, that you have a small space to fill between a paving slab and a wall. You could measure the space with a rule and transfer the measurements to the slab. But there is a better way, especially if the wall is not parallel with the last slab. What you should do is to place a fresh slab against the wall and overlapping the last slab laid (fig. 20). If the slab has a special upper surface (a grain finish, for example), *then it must be turned upside down.* Using a straight edge make a line along the slab over the edge of the slab beneath. In fact, to be precise, the line should be moved away from the slab beneath by the width of two joints, since you will have one joint between the two slabs and

another against the wall. While it may seem complicated, in practice it is quite simple. When laying the slab you turn it the right way up so that the edge which has been cut (and which is no longer parallel) faces the wall. This is always the best procedure when cutting lines that are off-square. If you have to accommodate a paving slab round a curved wall, the side of the pond for example, cut the curve first and then cut the opposite side using this overlapping method.

Concrete slabs

Pre-cast concrete slabs are perhaps the most commonly used paving material. They are cheap compared with many alternative materials. Their popularity is reflected in what appears to be an ever increasing choice as regards shape, colour, size and finish. Concrete slabs are cast in two ways: they are either vibrated or hydraulically pressed. Hydraulically pressed slabs are probably stronger, but this need only be a consideration if you intend driving a car over your patio. Typical sizes of concrete slabs are 300 mm and 600 mm square, and 300 × 600 mm. The thickness varies from about 40

Fig. 20. Marking a slab for cutting. If the wall is not running parallel with the edge of the slabs and the slabs have only one finished surface, it is essential that the slab is turned over before marking.

to 50mm. For motorised traffic a thickness of 100 mm or more is to be recommended. Interlocking slabs are popular. They are laid in exactly the same way as square or rectangular ones and should be no more difficult to cut. You can also buy square and rectangular slabs which are designed to form a repeating pattern. While attractive in their own right, consideration should be given as to whether the design will readily accommodate the straightforward shape of a pond. The so-called 'Dutch Pattern' (see fig. 21), for example, would require much cutting

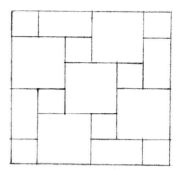

Fig. 21. The Dutch pattern made from paving slabs of three different sizes.

A variety of interlocking paving elements.

and on a small patio this could spoil the design. Concrete slabs are usually produced in bright, some would say, garish colours. While the basic colour will remain, the colorants usually fade to a much less vivid shade after a few months.

It is also possible to make your own concrete slabs. Glass-fibre moulds can be obtained for the purpose or you can make up forms from interlocking sections of wood. A colorant or pigment can be added to your concrete mix, but to obtain uniformity of colour in each mix it is essential that you use exactly the same proportions of sand, gravel and cement, as well as colorant each time. Even the amount of water you use will affect the density of the pigment. Mix cement, sand and gravel (consisting of particles no larger than 10 mm) in the ratio 1:2:3. Grease your moulds and the surface you intend turning them out on with soap, washing up liquid or paraffin. Fill the moulds with concrete and tamp well down. Then simply turn out the concrete like a jelly. Large slabs can be reinforced with chicken-wire. Making slabs for a patio of any size is a laborious job, but the saving in cost can be very considerable. Home-made paving slabs can be as little as a third of the cost of bought ones.

Bricks and tiles

Bricks, on the other hand, may cost several times as much as concrete slabs. Also the fact that they are much smaller, usually about 215 × 100 × 65 mm, means that one has a great many more to lay and the whole operation will take much longer. But bricks, mellowed with age, neither competing with, nor taking from, the beauty of more vivid plants, exert a charm all of their own. Bricks are a soothing and warm type of patio material which concrete can not rival. If you choose bricks make sure they are suitable for patio use. They must be impermeable and frost resistant. Special paving bricks, sometimes called paving setts, with bevelled edges are also available. The small size and simple rectangular shape of bricks means that they can be combined in a variety of patterns. Patterns or modules which are square or rectangular, such as 'basket weave' are particularly suitable for formal, geometric ponds and patios, as cutting can be avoided altogether, or certainly minimised. On the other hand, a pattern like 'herringbone' inevitably requires the cutting of many small triangular pieces. Cutting bricks into fractions is not easy and may involve much wastage.

A patio made with a combination of herringbone and circular pattern, in which the gully trap serves as the centre point of the circle.

Fig. 22. An effective pattern for a brick path.

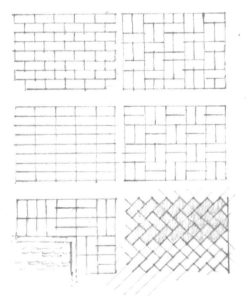

Fig. 23. A selection of brick paving patterns.

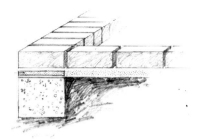

Fig. 24. *The outer line of bricks secured on a foundation of concrete and mortar. The inner lines of bricks can be laid on sand.*

Bricks can be laid on wet or dry mortar, or on sand. When using dry mortar or sand the bricks must be well bedded down. A small gap, about 10 mm, can be left for grouting. A wet mortar grout is very difficult to apply without staining the brick. Stains and efflorescence, the whitish deposits that sometimes appear on building materials on account of chemical salts, can be treated with patent cleaners or 10 per cent solution of hydrochloric acid. (Use these chemicals with care, wear gloves and avoid contact with the face. Keep well out of the way of children.) Dyes used in concrete or mortar may be affected by these cleaners, so always test on a spare piece of slab or a concealed corner. A dry mortar mix is more commonly used for bricks. Bricks can be consolidated by tapping into place or by a machine called a plate vibrator. Sweep dry mortar in between the bricks as you use the vibrator and then sweep the whole patio clean.

A brick patio must be held firmly in place

the whole way round. In the absence of a surrounding wall, the outside rows of bricks must be secured with a wet mix mortar on a concrete foundation. The foundation need only be the width or length of a single brick (depending upon which way the bricks are being laid) and about 15 cm deep, provided it is laid on firm sub-soil. It should be prepared as for the foundation of a pond (see page 23). Another way of securing the perimeter is by means of lengths of wood held in place with small stakes.

Bricks are in keeping with almost any patio design. But if you wish to highlight patterns in your patio, you might well choose tiles as your paving elements. While often as

A colourful patio garden. The pond is made of tiles with a rim of coarse grass. The patio is made of 'crazy paving' in situ concrete, i.e. the lines of the paving were marked in the concrete when wet. The seats are tiled in bright colours.

49

mellow as bricks, they can be much more vivid and nearly always have a more formal air about them. Again, it is important to make sure the tiles you choose are suitable for outdoor use. Bear in mind too that some tiles, particularly glazed ones, may tend to become slippery in frosty or even wet weather. Design possibilities are immense when one considers the range of tiles available. But do not make your pattern too complicated, not simply because of the difficulty of making a good job of it, but because the eye quickly grows tired of patterns that are too complicated. The thicker tile (50 mm and more) can

Fig. 25. Keeping tiles in a straight line is a problem. The best method is to lay each line against a straight edge.

be laid successfully on sand. Thin tiles are best laid in wet mortar. A useful way of maintaining an even line with tiles is by using a straight edge as a guide. Glazed tiles need to be very well laid. The fact that they reflect more than matt surfaces means they show up unevenness only too clearly.

Natural stone

The most lovely of all paving materials, by general consent, is natural stone. Flagstones in the company of an old house, an old twining rose and languid water-lilies with

perhaps the fragrance of honeysuckle somewhere about has no equal so far as patio gardening is concerned. Unfortunately the price of natural flagstones has no equal either. You can expect to pay, metre for metre, about the same price as a high quality, even a handwoven, carpet. Second-hand flags can sometimes be bought. It is worth checking with local builders and the columns of newspapers. You can make a considerable saving this way. An alternative is to be had in reconstituted stone which costs only about a quarter of the price of natural stone. Much of the cost of natural stone goes into cutting it into large, rectangular slabs which are known as cut stone. If the stone is more or less flat on one or both sides, it is sometimes referred to as dressed stone. Natural stone in random pieces, which make so-called 'crazy paving' is considerably cheaper. There is no

Natural stone is generally regarded as the finest of all paving materials.

50

An example of random stone used to make 'crazy paving'.

difficulty about laying crazy paving, but two points should be borne in mind. First of all, do mix in the large and small pieces as you go. The temptation is to use all the large pieces first with the result that the patio looks very unbalanced with all the large pieces at one end and the small ones at the other. Spread the large ones round. The second point is to make sure that you do not lay the crazy paving in obvious lines. There should be no 'seam' running through the joints, as can happen if you lay the pieces in obvious rows. Sand, dry or wet mortar (wet mortar is best if pieces are very small) can all be used as bedding. A long board and level can be used to maintain the fall of the patio or you may find using a builder's line stretched from one paving slab to another at some distance preferable. Metamorphic and sedimentary rocks are the usual source of natural paving stone. Having a grain, these rocks can be split and the surface then has an attractive riven finish. Riven stone usually varies a little in thickness so additional care is required to get the slabs level.

These methods of laying a patio are quite suitable for normal domestic use: foot traffic and small lawnmowers. But if your patio must also serve as a driveway, then a foundation of solid concrete is advisable. The concrete can be left bare or paving elements laid on top, using one of the methods already described, the dry and more particularly the wet mortar method being the most suitable.

In situ concrete

In situ concrete undoubtedly provides the most durable of all patios and requires

Fig. 26. When laying random paving pieces make sure the joints do not form an obvious line or seam as illustrated.

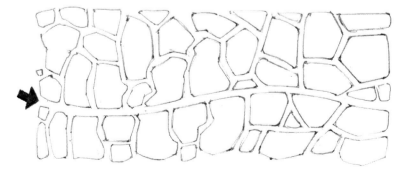

minimal maintenance. Natural flagstones laid on concrete are less vulnerable to cracking, as indeed are all materials. Glazed tiles can be laid more evenly on concrete. Use a lean mix concrete if you intend using it under paving slabs or sets: 1 part of cement to $3\frac{1}{2}$ of sand and 7 of coarse aggregate is suitable. If you buy the sand and gravel already mixed, what is known as all-in aggregate, then mix the cement in the ratio 1:10 (see also Appendix III). For an *in situ* concrete patio or driveway use 1 part of cement to 2 of sand and 4 of coarse aggregate; or in the ratio 1:6 for all-in aggregate.

It is not necessary to provide a base of

A novel garden scene which includes natural stone paving and small rectangular ponds, near which stand a large white sculpted fist, a terracotta pot of saxifraga and a clipped box shrub.

Pre-cast concrete units with an embossed pattern and coloured mortar make a lively patio.

Pigmented concrete being embossed with a stamper.

hardcore beneath the concrete unless your subsoil is liable to subsidence. In that case bed in coarse aggregate and a blinding of sand to a depth of about 100 to 150 mm. (The idea of the blinding is that it obliterates the unevenness and gaps in the hardcore, and so saves on the amount of concrete required.) As concrete is subject to contraction, it is necessary to lay it in sections (if it is going to be seen) and to insert fibreboard strips, which are made for the purpose, or use damp proof coursing (DPC). Softwood laths can also be used, indeed any material which separates the concrete into sections. No section of concrete should be longer than about 5 metres; or in the case of a narrow driveway or patio, the distance between joints should be no greater than twice the

width of the driveway. If slabs are to be laid over the concrete, a thickness of between 50 and 75 mm is adequate. But where the concrete itself constitutes the patio and when cars are concerned, make the concrete at least 150 mm thick. When laying down the concrete allow it to rise above the wooden sections. Then compact it down well and screed off any excess. If you have a large number of sections, lay the concrete in alternate sections on one day and then complete the job on a subsequent one. In this way it is possible to carry out the work without the problem of trying to avoid stepping on to wet concrete.

The surface of *in situ* concrete can be finished in a number of ways. Using a steel float provides the smoothest finish but this can be slippery. A wooden float will provide a slightly rougher finish. Before using a float allow the concrete to set a little. If there is water on the surface it will not be possible to obtain a proper finish. Instead of a float, a brush finish can be achieved by lightly brushing the surface with a yard brush. This brushed finish should not be confused with the exposed aggregate finish, which is obtained by using the same technique but with firmer, deeper strokes of the brush. An ordinary wooden board, placed across the shuttering and moved slowly with a sawing motion, will produce a rippled finish.

Concrete dyes can be added during the mixing or, more conveniently, can be added to the concrete after it has been laid. Companies that supply ready-mixed concrete are often reluctant to add dyes where small amounts of concrete are concerned. So pigments, such as Lithochrome, which are added after the concrete has been poured, are especially useful. The dye is supplied in powder form and is shaken on to the surface of the concrete and then worked in with a trowel and float. As the dye penetrates the concrete to a depth of several millimetres, it is permanent. It also has the effect of adding to the durability of the concrete. A Lithochrome wax is rolled into the concrete (preferably between eight and twenty-four hours after the concrete has been laid) to add brilliance to the finish.

Patterns can be made with concrete laid *in situ* in a number of ways. Timber sections, if made of redwood for example, can be left permanently in place, having first served as shuttering. The sections themselves can be of different sizes and shapes, or different sections can be given different finishes. You can add gravel to the surface of concrete as it sets and level it off with a board. This kind of finish, however, like cobbles, is not as pleasant to walk on as a smoother surface. A more sophisticated and varied method of finishing *in situ* concrete has been developed with much success in the United States. This is a professional method of embossing or printing concrete by means of a series of interlocking stampers. The impression of brickwork, for example, can be achieved at a fraction of the cost of real brick. Mortar can be added to the 'joints' to enhance the effect. This method of embossing concrete also has the advantage of covering any area without the trouble of cutting paving elements. Where manhole covers, circular and intricately shaped raised ponds and beds are concerned, this is a considerable advantage.

Having laid your patio by one of these methods and using one of the many materials available, you will almost certainly want to add some ornamental features. That is the subject of the next chapter.

Patio made of a combination of small cobblestones set in concrete and exposed aggregate (made by brushing concrete).

6 Patio features

If you have ever sat in the middle of an open space you will almost certainly appreciate how different that feels from sitting in a smaller space bounded by low walls. Somehow a sitter is more comfortable in surroundings which have an obvious but not overbearing definition. (Note how in public parks people usually lie near trees without, necessarily, availing of their shade.) A boundary of some kind not only defines the area of the patio, it also defines the area for the occupants.

A wall around the patio

Brick is surely the most satisfying building material with which to make a wall for the patio. Choose frost-resistant bricks known as 'ordinary' or 'special' quality. So-called engineering bricks are particularly durable. Calculate the number of bricks you need by dividing the length of the proposed wall by the length of a single brick plus the mortar joint. Then multiply that figure by the number of courses required. For example, let us say the wall is to be 20 metres in length, the brick 215 mm and the mortar joint about 10 mm (the brick can then be regarded as 225 mm long). Remember to convert the metres to millimetres by multiplying by 1000 or conversely dividing the millimetres by the same figure to convert to metres, before making the calculation 20 ÷ 0.225 = 89 bricks. That is the number for a single course.

The number of courses is then calculated. Let us assume that the wall is 1.2 metres high and the brick 75 mm with a 10 mm joint to make a total height for the brick of 85 mm. Then 1.2 ÷ 0.085 = 14 courses. The total number of bricks for the entire wall will be 89 × 14 = 1246.

To this number will have to be added sufficient bricks for supporting piers. An integrated pier extending out one side of the wall only will require at least one additional brick per course. A pier at the end of the wall will require at least four additional bricks per course; while a larger pier, of greater strength, suitable for heavy gates, would need six. Always fill the interior of gate piers with damaged bricks or rubble and mortar. Integrated piers are necessary to provide long walls with stability. Walls of great length should also be dry jointed at specific intervals. (Appendix III provides details and diagrams on the depth and width of foundations, the piers required and the allowable distance between dry joints for walls up to 1.8 metres high.)

Begin your wall by digging out the foundation to the required depth and width, using a builder's line (see page 23). Do remember that the width of the foundation must extend out either side of the wall. Right angles should be checked by means of a wooden triangle. Make up a triangle, the larger the better, with sides in the ratio 3:4:5. The triangle will then have one angle of 90°

also. If they are of equal length, then the corners must be at right angles. Drive pegs into the trench to obtain the proper level for the foundation. Mix cement, sand and coarse aggregate in the ratio 1:2½:5 by volume (see also Appendix III). Place in the trench up to the top of the pegs, tamp well down and allow to set.

For the brick laying, you will need mortar, that is cement and sand, in the ratio 1:6, to which is added a proprietary plasticizer. The value of the plasticizer is that it makes the mortar more pliable and workable. Use it according to the maker's instructions. Lime was once used extensively before the advent of plasticizers and is still used widely. It is cheaper but does not provide quite so workable a mix. If you use lime, the proportions of cement, lime and sand should be 1:1:6. Dry-mix mortar can also be bought in bags. If you need only small quantities this is a convenient way of buying mortar, but it is not economic for large amounts. Mix no more mortar than you can use before it stiffens noticeably. Ideally you will have someone mixing the mortar and carrying it on site while the brick building continues uninterrupted. Almost all building jobs are better carried out by two people. Building walls certainly falls into this category. When mixing the materials keep them free from any little stones that may be lying around. They can be very irritating as bricks will not sit properly if a stone is lodged underneath. Use a spot board for the mortar. It can be moved along as you lay each course.

Begin by laying out an entire course of bricks *dry*. This is most important in order to get the corners laid accurately as well as the bricks spaced evenly. Having done this, lay the corner bricks in mortar and then the intervening bricks. The method of brick laying is as follows: using a builder's trowel, lay down enough mortar for one corner brick (subsequently enough mortar can be laid down for several bricks at a time). Then depress the mortar with the point of the

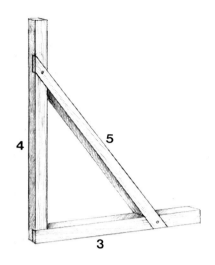

Fig. 27. Tools of the trade. Above: wooden triangle. Below: spot board; builder's level; straight edge; builder's trowel; flexible steel measuring tape; bolster chisel (with broad head); cold chisel (with narrow head), and club or lump hammer.

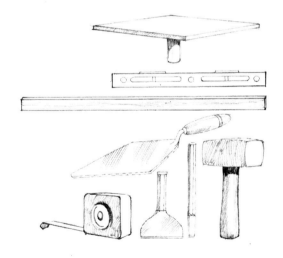

Building a patio boundary wall with piers.

trowel so as to almost divide the mortar into two lengths. You will find that the brick will settle down more readily if the mortar is divided in this way. Gently bed down the brick, remove surplus mortar squeezed out of the joint and slap it back down on the spot board. Use a level to see that the brick is perfectly horizontal. Next lay a brick at the far corner in the same way. Then stretch a builder's line from the top edge of one brick to the top edge of the other. Check that the line now forms a parallel with the opposing wall, if there is one; or check that it is at right angles with adjacent walls. Then lay the whole course of bricks using the builder's line as a guide. The procedure is the same as for the first two bricks, except that each brick must now be 'buttered' with mortar to make a joint with the brick next to it. The builder's line will enable you to keep each course level, but also use a spirit level to keep the wall vertical.

To obtain a strong and enduring wall it is essential that the vertical joints between the bricks are never placed directly above one another, but are 'staggered'. This is achieved most simply by beginning the corners of every alternate course with half bricks. By this means every joint is midway over the brick below. This is known as stretcher bond. If your wall is at right angles to another, it is not necessary to cut a half brick at that corner. Simply turn the last brick in alternate courses to run with the second wall. Bricks may be bonded in many ways. Fig. 28 shows a number of the more popular bonds. Double leaf walls are essential above 90 cm high if the material is brick. But even below that height, a double leaf wall is a decided advantage. It provides a sense of solidity which a single leaf wall lacks.

Both clay and concrete bricks may absorb salts from the surrounding soil and then secrete these salts, which appear on the brickwork as efflorescence. Providing the wall with a damp course (DPC), a sheet of bitumen felt or plastic as provided by any

Fig. 28. Bonds: **a** *stretcher bond, consisting of bricks laid lengthwise in each course, particularly suitable for single leaf walls;* **b** *English bond, alternate courses of headers and stretchers;* **c** *English garden wall bond, two or more courses of stretchers to one course of headers;* **d** *Flemish wall bond, one header with three stretchers on each course;*

e *Flemish bond, each course containing alternate stretchers and headers.*

Note the use of Queen Closers (a brick split in half lengthwise) in the corners to prevent alignment of joints and so increase the strength of the corners.

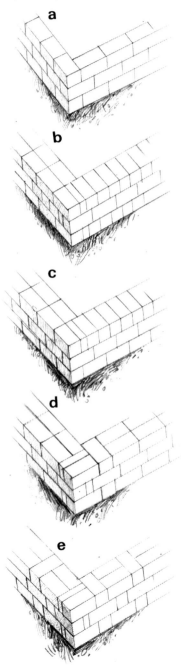

building merchant, is one remedy, the damp course is simply inserted into the wall during construction. Cement may also cause efflorescence, especially if an *in situ* concrete coping is used to finish the wall. The same remedy can be used at the top of the wall too.

All joints should be pointed. Fill up any gaps in the joints with mortar and carry out the pointing when the mortar has stiffened somewhat. Mortar which is soft will not provide a good finish. Probably the easiest way to point a wall is with a curved piece of pipe which is rubbed across the joints. Point the horizontal joints first and then the vertical ones. Pointing with a piece of pipe provides a concave finish to the joint. A flat finish, flush with the brick, can be obtained by using a trowel and a length of straight wood. The wood is held up against the wall and the surplus mortar 'cut' from either side of the joint with the trowel. There is something of a knack to this method and it takes longer than the method of rubbing with a curved pipe.

Fig. 29. Damp proof coursing (DPC).

Pointing a joint with a piece of rubber hose-pipe.

Raised beds and troughs

If you can handle bricks successfully – and the main advantage a skilled "brickie" should have over the newcomer is speed – a whole range of possibilities opens up. The most obvious is that of incorporating troughs in the wall for growing plants. In larger patios, free-standing raised beds are an option. Single-wall troughs or raised beds, especially if the bricks are laid on the flat, are quite strong enough to withstand the pressure of soil. Interlocking slabs of concrete, with decorative finishes such as exposed aggregate, can be bought and are readily assembled. These represent an alternative to constructing your own brick beds. Raised beds are a help to the disabled gardener, whose needs are discussed in Chapter 11. So far as plants are concerned 30 cm is a more than adequate depth of soil for anything except large shrubs and trees. Convenience and aesthetic considerations are more important as regards the precise height of raised beds. If possible do not concrete over the base of the bed or trough. This is particularly important if you live in an area with a high rainfall. If water cannot soak away, the soil in the trough may well turn sour and root rot can be a problem. Drainage holes should be incorporated in any troughs with a solid base. Either leave small holes in the mortar joints (leaving a stick between bricks until the mortar has almost set) or, for neatness, put in a series of small plastic pipes.

Bricks tend to absorb a good deal of the moisture from the soil in a trough. It is advisable to line each trough with polythene sheeting, especially in dry climates. The polythene must be perforated to prevent the soil becoming sodden; and the base should not be covered, at least not fully, unless you intend growing bog plants. Even in fairly damp climates such as is experienced in parts of Scotland and Ireland, it is surprising how quickly raised beds can dry out. At the same time these countries can experience rain over a sustained period. So the answer is to line your troughs with polythene, but imperfectly. The aim is to slow down the rate at which water is lost, rather than to prevent it.

Barbecues

A brick barbecue, either integrated in the wall or free-standing, can add much to a patio garden. There are three essential elements in a barbecue: the grill upon which

Raised bed made of pre-cast concrete sections.

the food is cooked; the grate underneath to support the charcoal or whatever fuel you wish to use; and a slab adjacent to the grill upon which kitchenware, knives, forks, plates, etc., can be placed. A barbecue can be made much more elaborate, of course, with cupboards, a chimney and rotating spit (manual or electric). But whatever you may devise, I suggest that the following points are worth observing. The grill should be not less than 700 mm from the ground, otherwise you will find yourself stooping unduly. For charcoal fires, the grill should be about 75 to 150 mm above the fire. It is a good idea to have an adjustable grill: simply insert flat metal supports between the courses of brick. The grill can then be slid out and on to a higher or lower level as necessary. Another way of controlling the heat is to allocate part of the grill to a sheet of metal, which will let

Filling a raised bed or trough with soil. Note the use of polythene to retain moisture. Make sure the polythene is very well perforated, as saturated soil will turn sour and may cause root rot.

The finished bed with fuchsia in the centre.

An attractive raised bed with evergreens.

*A well made patio of tiles and concrete slabs,
featuring a raised pond, garden
furniture and a barbecue.*

A built-in barbecue with cupboards.

not generate sufficient heat to cause problems with ordinary building materials. The concrete slabs for the grill base and for the utensils can be made in wooden moulds (in the same way as paving). Use a concrete mix of 1:2:3 and make the slabs 750 mm thick and reinforce with chicken-wire. The utensils slab can be tiled if desired. Designs for both integrated and free-standing barbecues are given in the illustrations on these pages.

Pierced screens

Brick is a material which can be used in almost any situation. There can be few surroundings where brick would not look well. The same is not equally true of pierced screen blocks which, most usually, require a modern setting. They are, however, very much cheaper than brick. Screen blocks vary in size, but 300 × 300 × 100 mm thick is typical. They are laid in much the same way as bricks. Use a mortar that is no stronger than 1:6, otherwise the cement could cause the blocks to crack.

Screen blocks are normally laid one directly on top of the other. Because the blocks are not staggered, the resulting wall has comparatively little strength. Above six courses the strength of the wall may be seriously impaired. Additional strength can be given to the joints by embedding small pieces of wire mesh. Screen block walls

less heat pass through than the bars. Food that is ready can be transferred to the metal plate while more food is being cooked.

There is an important point concerning the direction in which the bars of the grill are facing. This might seem irrelevant until you have actually cooked on a barbecue. If the bars are parallel with your chest, the only way food can be lifted with a spatula, is by sliding the spatula along the bars from left to right. This can be quite awkward for two reasons: the walls of the barbecue may obstruct your arm, and the most convenient way to use a spatula is not sideways but forwards. But this is only possible if the grill bars are running from front to back. If they do not, the spatula or any other utensil, will keep going between the bars.

Fire-clay bricks and heat-resistant concrete can be used in the construction of your barbecue, but an average charcoal fire will

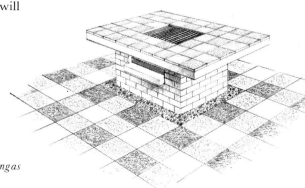

Fig. 30. A free standing barbecue with tiled top serving as a dining counter.

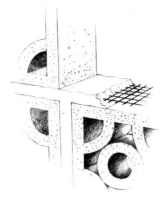

Fig. 31. The joints of perforated screen blocks can be strengthened by inserting wire mesh in the mortar.

require piers or pilasters inserted at intervals of about 2.7 metres or less. Obviously the higher the wall the shorter should be the interval. Take note of the specifications laid down by the manufacturer. Pilasters are usually designed so that the blocks can be slotted into them. When building the wall lay both pilasters and blocks together as a course. Do not attempt to make up the pilasters first and slot in the blocks afterwards, as this may weaken the joints. Instead of pilasters, ordinary concrete blocks or bricks can be used to form stabilising piers.

Shade for the patio

Screen blocks are not load-bearing. If you are fortunate enough to live in so sunny a climate that you feel your patio needs protection from the sun, any overhead covering must be supported by the pilasters or brick piers. Dappled shade can provide the most relaxing ambience. It can be achieved by lengths of thin wood, louvres as they are known, supported by rafters (joists) and beams. The closer the louvres are to one another, obviously the greater the shade. Remember that the width, *as opposed to the thickness*, of the louvres, rafters and beams should be set vertically. The danger of sagging is minimised in this way (see fig. 32). The beams will need to be about 100mm thick by 150mm wide. If screwed flat against a wall, a beam can be as little as 50mm ×

100mm. The rafters should be about 50mm × 150mm (lighter than the beams) and the louvres about 25mm × 100mm. The louvres will need to be supported by rafters at intervals of about 1200mm. If you use heavier material for the louvres the spacing of the rafters can be increased accordingly. The beams should be secured to the piers either by cementing in place or by using 'L' shaped brackets. Rafters and beams can be bracketed, slotted or 'toenailed' together (see below). Toenailing is the name given to inserting nails through the side of a length of wood as opposed to through the top. Louvres can be joined to the rafters by the same methods. However, with the toenail method it is difficult to space the louvres evenly.

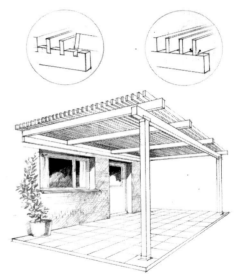

Fig. 32. Overhead shade provided by louvres. The louvres may be fastened to beams by joints (top left) or 'toenailing' (top right).

Whichever method you use, the spacing can be made much easier and more accurate by using small wooden blocks as you proceed. Supposing you want to space the louvres at 150mm apart. Then make a couple of wooden blocks 150mm thick. Secure the first louvre, then place the blocks up against it and the next louvre against the blocks.

A fine example of open brickwork.

Secure that louvre, remove the blocks and simply repeat the procedure. (If the blocks are square you will not have to concern yourself with choosing the right face to put against the louvre.) Blocks will not, of course, be needed if you use full saddle joints (see fig. 32). In this case what is needed is very accurate measuring. If desired the rafters can be omitted and the louvres secured directly to the beams. This means, however, that the beams must be at fairly close intervals; and more important, the louvres will now be at right angles to the house as opposed to parallel with it. Most people prefer the louvres running parallel to the house.

If you have no suitable pilasters or piers to support the beams, use wooden posts at least 100 × 100 mm thick. There are a number of ways in which the posts can be secured to the patio. They can be cemented in place, attached to angle fasteners if you have a concrete base, or secured to post anchors set in concrete. The advantage of angle fasteners and post anchors is that the posts can be replaced without disturbing the patio in any way.

Corrugated plastic (often reinforced with fibreglass) is another way of gaining protection from the sun. It differs from louvres in that it reduces the heat on the patio and cuts down on ultra-violet rays without creating any appreciable shade. The construction of the woodwork is slightly different for corrugated sheeting. In the first place the roof must have a pitch or slant away from the house. Building codes vary, but the pitch might be as much as 1 in 3. That is to say a roof which extends 3 metres from the house should be lower by 1 metre at the front. The spacing of the joists must be much closer than for louvres. The width of a single sheet, usually about 600 mm, is the appropriate spacing for the joists. You will also need cross members spaced the length of each sheet.

A raised patio with gently rising steps, and with outstanding planting around the perimeter.

Where the sheets are to be nailed to the timber frame, first nail on lengths of configurated wood moulding. Drill and secure the sheets with non-rust nails. You should be able to get special nails fitted with washers; these are best able to withstand high winds. Some nails are designed to take a plastic cap so as to prevent water leaking through. Make sure to nail the sheeting to the high point on the wood moulding and not in the dip, otherwise you are likely to damage the sheeting. Besides, a nail head in the groove

could cause water to collect at that point instead of running off. Each corrugated sheet should be overlapped by one groove.

Finally, if there is no overhang from house or wall to which you are attaching the roof, it will be necessary to secure flashing to the wall. This is to prevent rain getting down between the roof and the wall. Flashing consists of copper or aluminium sheeting which can be bought in rolled lengths of various widths, 300 and 600 mm being typical. The flashing is inserted between two

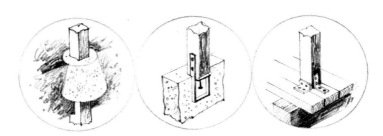

Fig. 33. Means of securing upright beams or posts.

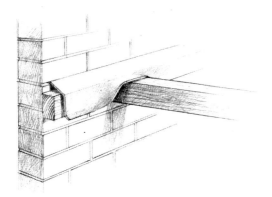

Fig. 34. *An example of flashing set in a wall to prevent water getting between the beam and the wall.*

courses of bricks to a depth of several centimetres and secured with mortar (see fig. 34). You will, of course, have to remove the old mortar from the wall first, using a chisel and hammer. The flashing is best put in place before the roof is put up. The wooden structure might not cause you much of a problem, but you will find that once the corrugated sheets are in place, it is almost impossible to work effectively on the wall above it. The same basic structure used for corrugated sheets can also be used for securing wooden boards over which asphalt sheeting, for example, can be laid. However, a solid roof will keep out a good deal of light and this is rarely desirable on a patio. The effect of louvres is unique to louvres.

Means of securing corrugated PVC with covered screws. Configurated wood moulding (not shown) attached to the top of the beam will reduce draught.

Steps

If your patio is lower than the entrance to the house or on a different level to the surrounding garden, you may find the need to make steps from one to the other. Steps consist of two parts: there is the tread, the part which is walked upon, and the riser, which separates and raises each tread from the one below. Bear in mind the following points when planning your steps: the width of the steps, for all practical purposes, should be not less than 750 mm, otherwise they will appear uncomfortably narrow. If space permits make them much wider. If the steps are going up to a door, then they should be at least as wide as the entrance (some building codes lay down certain minimum dimensions for particular situations). The tread from front to back should measure not less than 300 mm, but for a spacious effect the measurement would need to be closer to 450 mm. All treads should have exactly the same dimensions, as should the risers. It can be confusing and hazardous to negotiate steps of varying heights. Do think of steps in relation to the overall character of the patio. Generally speaking, if small, narrow and steep, steps tend to appear merely functional and not an attractive feature in their own right. Steps should be made as spacious as possible. That means the height of the risers must be small (to prevent steepness): between 100 and 150 mm will provide a gradual, accommodating ascent.

Steps, you will find, take up a great deal of space. Much more than you might imagine. Suppose, for example, that your patio is a full 1250 mm above a surrounding lawn, that you intend using pre-cast concrete slabs, 40 mm thick, for the treads; and bricks, 65 mm high, for the risers. The effective height of each riser will, in fact, be more than 65 mm. Not only must the height of the brick be considered, but also the thickness of the tread (40 mm) and the mortar joints above and below the brick, say 20 mm (2 × 10 mm). The effective height of each riser is therefore 65 + 40 + 20 = 125 mm. To calculate the number of risers required, divide the height of the patio by the height of one riser, i.e. 1250 ÷ 125 = 10 risers. In this instance the division produces a perfect whole number. Rarely are calculations with steps so obliging. Fractions cannot be accommodated because the steps must all be equal. The mortar joint will allow some latitude – it can be increased or decreased. But failing that, one has little choice but to use materials with different dimensions.

To calculate the depth of a flight of steps (the horizontal distance from the back of the top tread to the front of the lowest tread), multiply the number of treads by the depth of a single tread. Suppose the paving slab you are using is 450 mm deep, that is to say measured from front to back. Then from that figure must be subtracted the thickness of the brick riser, say 100 mm, plus the amount the slab overhangs the brick, say another 10 mm. Then the effective depth of the tread is 450 – 110 = 340 mm. The depth of the flight of steps can now be calculated as 10 × 340 = 3400 mm (see fig. 35). You can now appreciate just how much space steps tend to take up. It is always important to make your calculations on paper first. As often as not there simply is

not room to carry out first intentions and plans must be modified accordingly.

To make the steps, begin at the bottom, excavate the soil to accommodate the first paving slab (which should be a little below the level of the lawn to facilitate cutting) and work upwards. Bed down your first slab on sand or sand and cement. Then lay the first set of brick risers in mortar, add the next slab and continue on in this way. The treads should be allowed to slant forward very slightly so as to allow rainwater to run off. This method of making a flight of steps depends upon having an excavated site on which the treads are laid. It may well be that your steps will have no such support. In this case one either has to make brick walls to support the treads, or make *in situ* concrete steps which are then faced with whatever material one wants.

Steps can, of course, be made from *in situ* concrete and nothing else. Their making is laborious. One has to make up strong wooden formers to hold the concrete (see fig. 36). Aggregate and rubble can be used to fill up some of the interior space, but the concrete must not be less than 100 mm in any one place. To prevent the flight of steps sinking it may first be necessary to lay a concrete foundation. You can economise on this by simply digging out a few holes about 200 mm in diameter and of similar depth,

Fig. 35. Steps laid on an earth slope. The brick risers can be used on the front alone or at the sides of the tread as well.

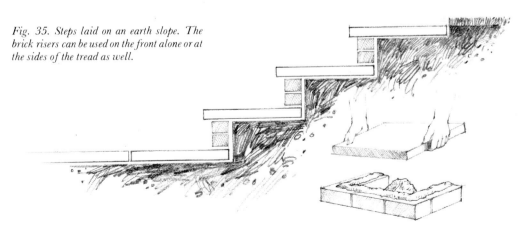

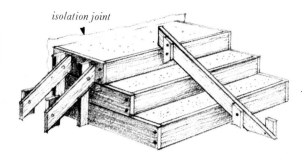

isolation joint

Fig. 36. In-situ concrete steps require carefully made shuttering. It is important to make an isolation joint between the steps and the wall.

beneath the bottom tread in particular. The concrete (consisting of cement, sand and aggregate in the ratio 1:2:3) must be very thoroughly compacted. Tamp down well and sharply tap the formers to expel bubbles from the concrete. Screed off excess concrete with a wooden plank and finish with a float and then a yard brush. Using only a float would provide a smooth finish which could be slippery. Indeed for safety reasons you might consider adding to the surface of each tread an abrasive such as silicon carbide. A point to remember, if you are making concrete steps against a wall, especially the wall of a house, is to make what is known as an isolation joint (see fig. 36). Simply insert a length of polythene or building paper between the wall and the concrete. The object is to prevent adherence and the risk that the wall might crack as a result. Concrete steps, it has to be said, are not nearly so appealing as those made of brick, slab or flagstone. However, where a single step of an awkward size is required or where the patio itself is made from *in situ* concrete, concrete has an obvious application.

Gates

Gates are a feature which are often added to patios. There is no difficulty about hanging gates provided a few points are observed. If it is a small, light wooden gate that you intend

hanging, then it can be attached to a wooden post sunk about 450 mm deep in concrete.

No small part of the attraction of a gate can be provided by the hinges you choose, of which there is a huge variety. Whatever hinge you choose, remember to leave an adequate space between the gate and post. Wood expands and a sticking gate is usually caused by the post and gate being too close together, or the post with the clasp for that matter. Set the gate up on two blocks and check with a spirit-level. Mark both gate and post for the screws and attach the hinges. Wrought-iron and gates of any weight are made with a heel which takes most of the weight when fitted into a circular iron disc. This must be set in concrete and set accurately. To do this set up the gate on blocks and with the heel in the iron disc. If the hinge at the top of the pier has already been secured, make certain the disc is low enough in the ground to allow the hinge to move freely. Make quite certain that the hanging stile of the gate is parallel with the pier, then concrete the disc in position.

Hanging a gate. Make sure the hinge is perfectly horizontal. Otherwise the gate may bind against the hinge.

Rustic poles make a cheap and easily constructed boundary to a patio.

Trellises and fences

If you are fond of working with wood a garden gate can be run up very easily. A gate should consist of at least two horizontal bars known as rails, a diagonal brace (to inhibit warping); two stout uprights or stiles at either end to take the hinges and clasp, and as many intermediate uprights or cladding as size and your design dictate. For a gate about 1100 mm long by 900 mm high, the rails and brace should not be less than about 100 × 20 mm, and the stiles about 75 × 50 mm. The cladding can be lighter. Mortise and tenon joints are the kind of joints the true woodworker relishes in making. For the less experienced very satisfactory joints can also be made by simply screwing the various members together, having applied a waterproof glue.

Wood remains an invaluable natural resource (although one we sadly tend to take for granted). It is still comparatively cheap. Bricks and pierced blocks we have discussed for building boundary walls. Wood offers an alternative that you might consider. Rustic poles can make an excellent trellis for climbing plants as well as providing a distinctive boundary for the patio, and they have another advantage. Rustic poles can make a wall or shield of considerable height, which, if made of bricks or blocks, might overpower a small patio. Moreover, there is no comparison in the cost or the labour involved. Rustic poles, obviously, are not suited to every situation. They would look decidedly odd, for example, if used as a wall dividing a front garden from a road. But dividing a patio from the rest of the garden they make a restful form of wall. Larch is often used for rustic poles as it endures and is not expensive. The uprights are best sunk in concrete, although simply digging a hole and tamping down with some aggregate may secure the pole well enough. In either case the poles should be sunk 450 mm if the trellis is to be 1500 mm high or more. The intermediate poles, horizontal or diagonal, can be arranged in an infinite variety of ways. But large, simple repeating patterns are usually more satisfactory than small, intricate, fussy ones. Unite the poles with long, sturdy nails. Though less often seen, presumably on account of the additional work involved, a formal trellis can be made from sawn and planed wood, such as redwood. If it is to look well, a formal trellis does require much more precise work and exact measurements. Any incongruity in a repeating pattern is immediately picked out by the eye. But a formal trellis wall has its virtues; not least is its comparative rarity. For this reason alone it can make a striking contribution to a patio.

Fig. 37. Three types of fencing. From top: simple post and rail fence; interwoven with trellis top (this type can often be bought in ready made sections); feather edge which has overlapping rails.

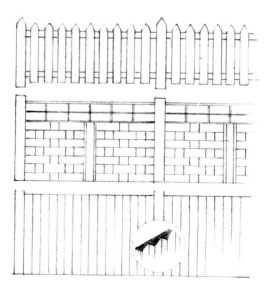

If privacy must take priority over design, then a fence could be substituted for rustic poles or a formal trellis. But I do not think fencing, however elaborate or imaginative, is ever as suitable as a patio boundary. It nearly always has a utilitarian air about it. Moreover, a see-proof fence involves a great deal of wood and can be expensive. A problem with all see-proof fences, except for the louvre type, is that they must be able to withstand a great deal of wind pressure. Open-work fences will at least let a proportion of any gale through, although it can be said that all fences are liable to gale damage. Use thick uprights, not less than 100 mm square, and space them at close intervals, certainly not more than 2 metres apart if the fence is more than 1300 mm high. The construction of a fence is very similar to that of a gate, indeed they can be identical in every detail. Use mortise and tenon or lap joints to joint the uprights with the horizontals. Sectional fencing can be bought and simply set in the ground as required. But whether you buy your fencing or make it yourself, be sure to use a builder's line and level when erecting the fence. A fence that does not follow a straight line or is of uneven height looks awkward no matter how intricate the design. All wood that is below ground level should be soaked in a preservative. Above ground level one has the choice between a preservative or paint. For a bright finish, paint is the obvious choice. But repainting a fence involves a certain amount of care and trouble. Applying or re-applying a preservative is a task which can be done quickly and at any time.

There is yet another way of making a boundary for a patio. That is with a hedge, and this is discussed at the end of Chapter 9. We have discussed the construction of both ponds and patios and the materials that one might use. It is now time to consider first water-lilies and the planting of the pond, and then planting the patio.

7 Clear water & water-lilies

Many people are apparently put off ponds by the belief that water must inevitably become stagnant and the only answer is continuous draining and replenishing the pond with fresh water. This simply is not true. Not only is it unnecessary to keep changing the water, it is positively harmful. Water-lilies much prefer to be left undisturbed. Currents swirling round the pool would inhibit the flowering of water-lilies; and neither they nor ornamental fish relish the sudden change of temperature that usually accompanies changing the water.

When you fill a new pond the water will, inevitably, turn a murky green. What has happened is this. A variety of micro-organisms, known collectively as algae, feed upon nutrients in water and multiply at vast speed until every cubic centimetre of water contains many thousands of algae blooms. Then the water is coloured, of course, and one can see nothing at all under the surface. How to get rid of these unsightly but harmless algae is quite simple. If you deprive the algae of their nutrition, they will simply die off, leaving the pond absolutely clear. You can do this in two ways. Algae are as dependent upon sunlight as on nutrients in the water. The pads of water-lilies, *Nymphaea*, stretching across the surface of the water cast useful shadows into the depths below. What is much more important is that you must introduce into your pond underwater plants, which will compete with — and defeat — the algae in an unequal struggle for salts and minerals in the water. These underwater plants are commonly known as 'oxygenators'. They are the essential ingredient in keeping pond water clear. There is a large range of tender and hardy underwater plants (many of which are notoriously difficult to identify, even for a botanist who has specialised knowledge of the subject), but it does not much matter which underwater plants you choose, although some plants will do better than others, depending upon the nature of the water in your pond. The best thing is to introduce two or three different types, one or more should flourish. Underwater plants can be collected in the wild. Any plant which produces underwater leaves (as opposed to merely starting growth under water to rise clear of the surface later) will serve the purpose. The problem with collecting plants from a local canal or natural pond is that you cannot be certain that the plants are free of pests. An aquatic stockist is a safer approach.

Typical of plants sold by aquarists and water garden centres are the following. *Elodea canadensis* (Canadian Pondweed, Ditch Thyme), which resembles a bushy green pipe cleaner. It produces tiny white flowers at the end of thin white threads. So minuscule are these flowers that they can pass unnoticed unless you look for them. *E. canadensis* is a vigorous plant and very efficient at keeping water clear. *Egeria densa*, which is very similar in appearance, has a three-petalled

The tiny red (and yellow) flowers of the Spiked Water Milfoil, Myriophyllum spicatum, rising above the water – in the presence of a healthy looking frog.

flower (nearly the size of a small finger nail), is rather less vigorous and is often preferred for that reason. *Myriophyllum spicatum* (Spiked Water Milfoil) is a splendid plant in every way. It has a delicate, feathery appearance, produces tiny but distinctive red and yellow flowers just clear of the surface, and is a quite excellent purifier, as is *M. verticillatum* which is a rather lighter green and favours calcareous water. The Water Violet, *Hottonia palustris*, has widespread but localised distribution. It produces purple or white flowers held high above the surface. An attractive plant but often difficult to establish. The Water Crowfoot, *Ranunculus aquatilis*, produces both underwater and floating leaves (which are quite different in appearance), and scores of dainty white flowers. It can quickly spread over the surface of a pond and would need to be kept in check where space is limited. In water where neither *Elodea canadensis* nor *Myriophyllum spicatum* do particularly well, I have got *Potamogeton crispus* (Curled Pondweed) to flourish. It has broad, crimped leaves of green or bronze and is not unlike seaweed. Fish like it, but from an ornamental point of view this plant looks rather untidy. There is much to be said for choosing an underwater plant which does not break the surface.

Ceratophyllum demersum and the less well known *C. submersum*, which have their leaves in attractive whorls (similar to *Myriophyllum spicatum* but stiffer) will leave the surface of your pond unbroken. All these oxygenators are hardy. Tender oxygenators include the Tape Grass, *Vallisneria spiralis*, which is commonly grown in aquaria; the lovely and well named Parrot's Feather, *Myriophyllum proserpinacoides*, which has foliage of the most vivid green. It likes to weave its way in and out of the water. *Cabomba aquatica*, a Mexican plant which produces small yellow flowers above the surface, has found wider distribution through pond keepers, although *C. caroliniana*, with its fan-shaped underwater leaves and elongated floating ones, is still the more popular form.

Most ponds will have to be filled with tap water. This should be perfectly satisfactory; simply leave it for a few days to allow the chlorine to evaporate. Oxygenators can be planted in shallow pots with a little loam. Snipping a few centimetres off the top of a stem and planting it in the soil is all that is needed for many plants, as most will establish roots very readily. 'New' water will be in an 'eutrophic' or mineral-rich condition. As a result the algae will thrive initially. This is both natural and inevitable. A period when the water is an unattractive, murky shade of green (harmless to fish, incidentally, who actually eat algae) must be endured in the knowledge that as the oxygenators become established and the water becomes 'oligotrophic' or mineral-deficient, the algae will disappear. It may take weeks or even months for the condition of the water to change. But once the process of clearing starts, the transition from murky green to crystal clarity is accomplished in only a matter of days. The question as to how many oxygenators a given pond may need is difficult to answer. As a rule, if a quarter of the pond *appears* to contain underwater plants that should be sufficient; but so far as clarity is concerned you cannot have too

A pond showing the bronzed elliptical floating leaves of Potamogeton natans, much favoured by spawning fish but rather vigorous for a small pond.

many plants. Once clarity is obtained it should remain permanent, except perhaps in early spring when algae may start into growth more quickly than the dormant underwater plants. Blanket weed (which is a type of alga) may form in the best kept ponds. Removal by hand, or twirled up on the end of a stick is the best answer. Your pond will never become stagnant so long as oxygenating plants are present and decaying leaves are absent. Nothing is likely to pollute a pond more quickly than leaves. Net the pond during the fall if necessary or remove all dead foliage by hand at regular intervals.

There is a curious idea that a pond must be of a certain minimum size otherwise the water will never clear or cannot be guaranteed to remain clear. This is another myth. The smallest patio pond can be as clear as a crystal lake. There is no minimum size as such, but there are other factors which should be noted. The ratio betweeen surface area and depth is very important. The deeper the pond — or the greater the volume of water, which amounts to the same thing — in relation to the surface area, the more easily can the clarity of the water be maintained. For this reason, a shallow, saucer-shaped pond should be avoided at all costs simply because that shape provides the maximum surface area with the minimum amount of water. When it comes to choosing plants for the pond, many water garden centres recommend a selection of water-lilies and other plants suited to your size of pond, and such selections can represent a saving, as opposed to buying individual plants; but if you want to make your own selection, there are various points to bear in mind.

Nymphaea are most usually grown today in plastic baskets with perforated sides. For hardy water-lilies these baskets range in size from about $30 \times 30 \times 20$ cm to $25 \times 25 \times 15$ cm and $20 \times 20 \times 10$ cm. These sizes correspond roughly to the vigour of the various water-lilies being grown, which are usually divided into vigorous, medium and small. Each category merges into the other (the vigour of plants is never precise) and at each end of the scale there are very vigorous plants and pygmy ones. If you have a tiny pond then the smallest basket will have to be used. Otherwise use one of the larger ones. So far as any water-lily is concerned the basket cannot be too large, for all *Nymphaea* are gross feeders.

Before being submerged in the pond, a lily is planted in soil in a basket lined with hessian. Pea gravel on top will prevent fish from disturbing the soil.

Line each basket with hessian or rags to retain the soil. The top spit from prime pastureland is generally regarded as the finest soil in which to grow water-lilies. That is cold comfort to the town gardener. In fact *Nymphaea* will thrive in any heavy loam, especially if fortified with bone-meal added at the rate of a handful or thereabouts to each basket. Only buy sterilised bonemeal and handle only with gloves as it can carry disease. Well rotted cow manure (particularly if layered with loam and left under cover for several months) is probably even more effective than bonemeal when applied at the same rate. However, you run the risk of enriching the water as well as the soil, in which case the algae may thrive and cloud the water for many months. A cleaner method and one which does not run the risk of fouling the water is to use a slow release fertilizer such as 'Plant-Gro'. You simply tuck the pellet into the soil under the tuber or plant. Water-lilies are best transplanted during the growing season. Spring is the most suitable time, since it gives the plants the best chance of getting established. A mature lily may well flower in its first season. Plant the tuber so that the growing point (from which leaves should be emerging) is pointing more or less vertically. On no account should the growing point be smothered in soil: leave it slightly exposed. Some gardeners add pea-gravel to the top of the soil to prevent fish snuffling for food and so clouding the water. The basket is lowered gently on to the bottom of the pond, or placed on bricks if the depth is too great. (If using bricks or blocks make sure they are well weathered. In a small pond fresh lime seeping from such materials can be fatal to plants and more especially fish.) Young tubers, in particular, are best started near the surface and gadually lowered as their leaves develop. An indication that a plant is too deep is seeing several leaves unfurl fully before reaching the surface. The strongest *Nymphaea* should have anything between 75 cm and 1 metre of water over their crowns; plants of medium vigour do best in between 45 and 60 cm; and the small and miniature lilies should have only a few centimetres up to about 30 to 45 cm. Unless your pond has a surface area in excess of 3.25 square metres it is not advisable to grow the more vigorous forms. Indeed really vigorous forms, such as the white 'Gladstoniana' or the red 'Charles de Meurville', require considerably more space. In a small pond they will simply spread their broad leaves over all the available surface area, giving the pond the impression of being cluttered. Vigorous lilies do not necessarily produce more flowers (in fact some produce less), all one is talking about is the size of the flowers and leaves and the rate of growth. Medium and small water-lilies will look far more congenial in a setting of limited size. Equally, if not more important, is the need to grow your plants in an adequate depth of water. If there is one fault more common in water gardening than any other it is having lily leaves heaping up on each other. The effect is hideous and quite at odds with the water-lily's greatest virtue: its sense of peace and repose. The leaves should float on the surface of the water and not rise above it.

It was a Frenchman, M. Latour Marliac, working in the South of France way back in Victorian times, who was the first man to achieve cross fertilization of hardy *Nymphaea* in a systematic way. He also started a fashion for ornamental ponds which has continued to grow to the present day. As his large output of hybrids spread across the world, names tended to become interchanged and some were given new names. This point is worth mentioning because it is not uncommon to find different nurseries growing the same water-lilies under different names.

The smallest white water-lily is the dainty *Nymphaea pygmaea alba* whose flowers one can encircle between thumb and forefinger. Its leaves are a lighter shade of green than most water-lilies. *N. tetragona* is another white miniature, very similar to *N. pygmaea alba*

N. x *Marliacea 'Chromatella'*

though somewhat larger. *N. candida* is a larger plant again, suitable for medium size ponds. When Marliac was particularly pleased with a hybrid he had produced, he attached the Latinised form of his name to the plant. *N.* x *Marliacea* 'Albida' is a splendid plant which flowers exceptionally well, but it is vigorous and requires a good deal of space. *N. alba* 'Candidissima' — not to be confused with *N. candida* — has wonderful double flowers of pure white. Again it is a plant that needs space. Equally desirable is *N.* 'Gonnère' which has immense double flowers and is slightly less vigorous than *N. alba* 'Candidissima'.

Among yellow water-lilies, the American *N.* 'Sunrise' has perhaps the richest shade of all, and it is suitable for medium size ponds. Of similar vigour, but producing flowers of a more delicate yellow, is *N.* x *Marliacea* 'Chromatella'. Somewhat less vigorous is *N.* 'Moorei', which is very similar indeed to *N.* 'Chromatella', having leaves blotched with purple, and an abundance of yellow flowers of similar hue, but *N.* 'Moorei' is a slightly smaller plant. So far as tub and tiny ponds are concerned there is one obvious choice for a yellow lily and that is *N. pygmaea* 'Helvola'. It is impossible not to feel a special affection

N. 'Helvola' is ideal for the small pond. It is very prolific with its flowers.

for this plant if you have grown it for even a single season. It seems to be more spirited than any other miniature water-lily. At the slightest sign of spring weather it breaks into leaf and flowers profusely all summer and seems reluctant to give up in autumn. You will often find too that *N. pygmaea* 'Helvola' will flower under adverse conditions when other lilies are not flowering at all. If you are partial to star-shaped blooms then *N.* 'Solfatare' is an excellent choice for the small pond. The blooms open with a hint of yellow and become an increasingly darker shade of pink with age. The foliage is conspicuously mottled with maroon. This characteristic of blooms to darken — or lighten — with age and even to alter colour belongs to several lilies. Normally a bloom might be expected to last three or four days. On each day a change in the bloom will be apparent. *N.* 'Aurora' opens yellow and becomes red, having passed through a stage of orange. *N.* 'Graziella' does almost the opposite, opening a reddish yellow and becoming lighter. All these lilies are suitable for small ponds. *N.* 'Paul Hariot', with apricot yellow flowers becoming darker with age, and the slightly more vigorous *N.* 'Indiana', with its blotched foliage and orange red flowers, are suitable for medium and small ponds.

As far as red lilies are concerned, for the small pond you can hardly do better than choose a hybrid bearing the name *Laydekeri*. That is the Latin form of Maurice Laydeker, Marliac's son-in-law. All lilies bearing his name are ideal for small ponds. *N.* x *Laydekeri* 'Purpurata' with its crimson flowers (sometimes flecked with white) is among the smallest and most prolific. *N.* x *Laydekeri* 'Lilacea' does not have flowers that are exactly lilac in shade, rather they are soft rose hue with a hint of lilac. *N.* x *Laydekeri* 'Fulgens' is somewhat similar with more crimson in the flowers and bearing bright red stamens. *N. pygmaea* 'Rubra' is rather larger than the white or yellow pygmy lilies, but the fact that it is not a strenuous grower makes it

N. 'Solfatare'

quite suitable for growing in tubs. For a medium-sized pond you might choose *N. odorata* 'W. B. Shaw', an unusual lily in that its pink flowers are darker on the outside than inside, while *N.* x *Marliacea* 'Rosea' and the extremely delicate pink of *Marliacea* 'Carnea' are outstanding choices for the larger pond. *N.* 'Wilfron Gonnère' is another hybrid raised by Marliac. It has semi-double blooms of rich pink which to some growers resemble camellia blooms. It is suitable for the medium to large pond. One of the most vivid (and delicate) pink water-lilies — and for many the finest hybrid for the medium-sized pond — is the American *Nymphaea* 'James Brydon'. It bears distinctive cup-shaped flowers formed from many petals. An adaptable plant, it will tolerate shade better than most. It is reliable without being prolific.

Among red lilies, by general consent, *N.* 'Escarboucle' is the finest of all. It bears magnificent blooms up to 20 cm across — indeed they can be larger under optimum conditions — of the richest hue. *N.* 'Gloriosa', particularly popular in America, runs 'Escarboucle' close. Both require a fair amount of space. *N.* 'Attraction', with star-shaped red flowers, is a good choice for medium-sized ponds. My own favourite small red water-lily is *N.* 'Froebeli'. It has less petals than *N.* x *Laydekeri* 'Purpurata' (which it

N. x *Marliacea* 'Carnea'

N. x *Marliacea* 'Rosea'

resembles), but I love Froebeli's neat cup-shaped flowers often held several centimetres above the surface of the water. The blooms are a conspicuous shade of hot red unlike 'Escarboucle'. *N.* 'Froebeli' is comparable to *N.* 'Helvola' in the length of its flowering season. It prevails against the colder days of autumn better than any lily I have grown.

The cold winds of autumn will not concern those living in frost-free, sub-tropical areas such as the Southern states of the USA, California and Australia. The tender *Nymphaea*, which can easily be grown in such places, are exotic plants possessing blooms of the most extraordinary shape and hue. Readily hybridised, there are many hun-

N. 'Attraction'

dreds if not thousands of different tropical water-lilies now in cultivation. There is no hardy blue water-lily. Among tender lilies there is a vast tonal range of blues, from the palest shade to the darkest shade imaginable. *N.* 'Blue Smoke', of medium vigour, has flowers of the lightest blue, while *N. colorata*, a pygmy tropical, is close to navy blue. If purple takes your fancy then you might choose the brilliant *N.* 'Mrs. Martin E. Randig', a vigorous grower, or *N.* 'Royal Purple' which is suitable for the smallest pond. Among pinks, *N.* 'General Pershing' of medium vigour has long been a special favourite. It was produced by the fine American lily breeder, George H. Pring, and it has flowers of the most gorgeous pink. Martin E. Randig produced a most rare plant in *N.* 'Green Smoke' which, as its name would suggest, has green petals — which turn to blue at the tips. The blooms of all hardy water-lilies respond to sunlight, opening only during the hours of daylight and then for only the warmest and brightest part of the day. Not the least of the virtues of some tender lilies is that they open at dusk and remain open during the hours of darkness. If you use your patio at night, especially for barbecue parties, this is a boon. *N.* 'Missouri', another hybrid of G. H. Pring's, has large white blooms and flowers at night. It does require a good deal of space. Another old favourite and one which requires less space is *N.* 'Mrs. Emily Grant Hutchings', which has flowers of coral pink.

Tropical water-lilies are even more greedy in their soil requirements than are the hardy ones. A basket 30 cm deep by 60 cm square is not at all too big, and the soil should certainly be reinforced with cow manure and bone

meal to obtain the best results. Unlike the hardy forms, the tender lilies should only have about 15 to 20 cm of water over their crowns. It is customary to lift, thin and replant tropical lilies annually as they tend to grow very rapidly indeed. Few tender lilies will do well in water whose temperature is not consistently above 21°C. For this reason the UK and much of the European continent is only likely to produce, at best, erratic results with tender water-lilies. They can sometimes be grown in a conservatory if conditions are favourable. In any case, the best method under less than ideal circumstances is to treat tender lilies as annuals, removing the tubers or 'eyes' for overwintering indoors. Young, immature tubers are easier to keep than mature tubers during dormant months. The tubers should be stored in damp sand which is exposed to the free circulation of air, but protected from rodents which are very partial to them. A low temperature, 10-15°C., is best. Once warm weather returns in the spring the tubers can be planted and started in a greenhouse if available. *N. stellata*, which bears light blue flowers, is a good choice if your climate is a borderline case for tender lilies, and the night-flowering *N. caerulea*, also light blue, will flower in lower temperatures than most.

Two other deep-water aquatics at the

opposite end of the scale to tender lilies, so far as climate is concerned, deserve mention. The Water Hawthorn, *Aponogeton distachyus*, will flower right through the year until the first frosts and sometimes beyond. It is by no means uncommon to see this attractive plant in flower in Britain in December and January. It is obliging as regards depth too, thriving in as little as 15 cm of water and up to at least 60 cm. It is, however, slow to become established. Water Hawthorn has dark green strap-shaped leaves and long boat-shaped flowers of pure white with black anthers. The perfume resembles that of the Hawthorn tree although it has to be said that, as with *Nymphaea*, one has to approach the Water Hawthorn fairly closely to become aware of its fine perfume. The other plant is rather like a miniature water-lily with yellow trumpet flowers: *Nymphoides peltata* will grow in any depth of water up to 90 cm. Its leaves are only a few centimetres across, so it is ideal for the tub and small pond. It does spread quickly but there is no difficulty about removing surplus leaves as necessary.

You might also like to include a floating plant or two. Floating plants need only be placed in the water, after which they fend for themselves. Some, if they come close to soil in shallow water, will send down roots and become anchored at that spot; but for the most part floating plants float freely on the surface of the pond during the summer months, taking all necessary nutrition from the water. The tiny and delicate Ivy-leaved Duckweed, *Lemna trisulca*, is worth having for its miniature ivy-like fronds 'holding hands', as it were — it is said to be beneficial in keeping water clear. The other duckweeds, such as the prolific *Lemna minor*, the Lesser Duckweed, which is found on countless waterways, can be a nuisance, although fish usually keep it down to manageable proportions. No such solution is possible with *Azolla caroliniana* which will cover the surface of a pond as effectively as a carpet will cover a floor, though it has to be admitted that its

green sward in summer and russet hue in autumn is most spectacular. The lovely Frogbit, *Hydrocharis morsus-ranae*, has kidney-shaped leaves not much larger than a thumbnail and conspicuous white flowers. Like most floating plants, Frogbit winters on the bottom of the pool, but not in its summer form. It produces little stolons which nestle in the mud before developing in the following spring. For this reason Frogbit must be transferred to a bowl or another pond before the autumn, if you intend cleaning out the pond during the dormant period. *Stratiotes aloides*, or Water Soldier, resembles nothing so much as the spiky top of a pineapple. A most impressive plant, it thrives only in calcareous water, and spends a comparatively short time on the surface each year, when it produces a solitary white flower held high above the water. But I do not suppose there is any dispute as to which is the finest of all floating plants — that must be the Water Hyacinth, *Eichhornia crassipes*, which floats balloon-like on an inflated 'petiole' or stalk. Its bright green leaves are most striking, as are its lilac blue flowers each with its yellow eye. The Water Hyacinth is tender, as is the Water Lettuce, *Pistia stratiotes*, whose leaves are an extraordinarily vivid shade of light green.

Water-lilies suffer from few complaints. You might come across a phenomenon known as fasciation, but it is rare. For some unknown reason some hybrid lilies suddenly produce a large number of tiny leaves and no flowers. The only solution is to select a part of the tuber which is unaffected and cut away all other parts of the plant. The good tuber is then replanted. A fungus of the genus *Cercosporae* is also rare. The symptoms of this fungus are spots on the leaves which become dry and crumpled. (Spots often develop on decaying leaves; that in itself is no indication of fungus — it must be accompanied by the other symptoms as well.) Remove affected leaves and spray lightly with Bordeaux mixture at half the strength recommended

A well planted sunken pond with random stone paving and a brick bridge.

pygmy ones, are water snails of the *Limnaea* genus. They are easy to identify but much harder to eradicate. If the snail has a conical shell, then it is a *Limnaea* and it is likely to feed hungrily off the leaves of small water-lilies to such an extent that the plants cannot establish themselves and simply rot away. Pick out these snails when you see them or try placing a few crushed lettuce leaves in the pond overnight. The snails gather on the leaves and can be removed in the morning.

These few problems apart, water-lilies and most aquatic plants are very robust. You should enjoy their growth and blooms over many years. Lift the lilies every few years when growth is becoming too dense or when they are obviously in need of richer soil, and divide and replant. From *Nymphaea* and deep water aquatics we can now turn our attention to so-called marginal plants and plants for the patio.

For many the finest of all floating plants is the Water Hyacinth, Eichhornia crassipes. It is, unfortunately, tender.

for other plants. Bordeaux mixture should not be used in the presence of fish.

A much more common problem so far as water-lilies are concerned is the arrival of insects at your pond. Some of the more troublesome ones are bound to arrive sooner or later. Aphids, especially the Water-lily Aphis *Rhopalosiphum nymphaeae)*, the larva of the China Marks Moth *(Nymphula nymphaeata)* and Caddis flies *(Trichoptera)* will all feed voraciously off lily leaves and in some instances their tubers too. Keep fish. That is the best answer, and Golden Orfe, young and energetic, are best of all. They will keep the insect population down to reasonable proportions. In the case of very bad infestations of these insects, you can bath your plants in Derris solution, but this compound is highly toxic to fish, so great care must be taken in washing off all the Derris from your plants before returning them to the pond. Another scourge of water-lilies, at least young plants and more particularly the

As well as 'Attraction' (red) and 'Albida' (white) water-lilies, this pond includes the Parrot's Feather, *Myriophyllum proserpinacoides (left) and Bulrush (Typha) on the right.*

8 More plants for the pond

There once was a time when a visitor to a great estate might hear, not long after dawn, the clink of many garden forks and spades. Then, rising a few hours later, the visitor would see beneath his window a whole array of freshly planted flowers in full bloom. The process might be repeated many times during the growing season.

That day is gone; but the practice of rotating water plants as they go out of bloom with those coming into bloom is within the scope of the water gardener, even if dawn is not the preferred time. Today water plants are usually grown in plastic pots (similar or indeed the same as for *Nymphaea*, the larger the better). If you have a spare corner in your garden, hidden from general view, then it is an easy matter to dunk a few pots in an old tub or zinc bath. Then when those plants are about to burst into bloom they can be transferred to the pond, a process which should only take minutes. Since most patio ponds are small there is a limit to the number of plants that can be accommodated. This practice extends the range.

Marginal plants or bog plants differ in their water requirements. Some like the soil no more than damp and will not tolerate their roots being constantly sodden. Others thrive when their roots are below water level.

Planting or lifting a marginal basket, in this case containing a Marsh Marigold, Caltha palustris, takes only a minute or two.

You will want to conceal your baskets by having the rim a few centimetres below water level, so the marginal plants best suited to patio ponds are those that actually grow in water. Line perforated baskets with hessian or old rags and fill with garden soil. Marginal plants should only be planted when they are in active growth.

To begin the flowering season right at the beginning of spring, you should grow the dainty but robust little Bog Bean, *Menyanthes trifoliata*, which has exquisite little white flowers with tiny white hairs on each petal. This prostrate plant likes to spread about in an informal way, so it is a useful plant for softening a rectangle or a corner. Equally informal is the Marsh Marigold, *Caltha palustris*, which produces an abundance of very bright yellow flowers over a long period. It grows only about 20 cm high. It is supposed to be the plant that Shakespeare describes as the 'winking May-bud with golden eye'. *Caltha* is also known as Kingcup, but I like the Italian name best: 'Sposa di Sole' – Spouse of the Sun. Legend has it that if you wear Kingcup on your person, you will be immune to angry words. There is a double form, *C. palustris flore plena*, and a smaller white form, *alba*, about 15 cm high, from the Himalayas. Grow them all and you will extend the flowering season, as the different forms are likely to open at different times. Another spring-flowering plant is the Golden Club, *Orontium aquaticum*, whose flowers are like yellow-tipped matchsticks with pure white stems. The leaves are exceptional too: green on the upper side, silvery beneath. Watch the shimmering effect this produces in even a gentle breeze. This plant requires more soil than most, and a basket 30 cm deep is necessary.

You will almost certainly want to grow a few irises. Easily the most obliging is *Iris sibirica*, which is happy in a herbaceous border or standing in water (but with no more than 10 cm of water over its crown). It is a most reliable plant and is available in many

The crested flower of the Bog Bean, *Menyanthes trifoliata*.

The flower of the double Marsh Marigold, *Caltha palustris flore plena*.

Iris sibirica 'Tropical Night'

shades of blue, as well as in white and red. Container grown, *Iris sibirica* reaches a height of about 65 cm. Another favourite is the water iris, *I. laevigata*, also available in a number of shades, but the type is the equal of any in having striking flowers of very dark, rich blue. Similar in appearance to *I. laevigata* is *I. kaempferi*. The plants can be distinguished, however, by running a finger along the centre of their leaves: *I. kaempferi* is the one with the distinctive raised rib. Distinguishing between them is important because *I. kaempferi* favours acid soil, fortified with cow manure if possible, and while it likes plenty of water during the growing season, dampness rather than saturation is preferred during the winter. *I. kaempferi* is not as reliable a flowering plant as, say *I. sibirica*,

but to see its broad, flowing petals seemingly afloat on the summer air is to love this plant. The 'Higo' strain of *kaempferi* is a double form with six petals in place of the customary three. The iris has had an elevated history. In ancient mythology, it was believed to have descended from the rainbow, for the rainbow contains no greater variety of colour. Certainly a selection of irises in bloom in the height of summer is a brilliant and thrilling sight.

For the larger pond, the Yellow Flag, *I. pseudacorus* and its variants, 'Bastardi' (which bears lemon yellow flowers) and 'Variegata' (with boldly striped leaves), and *I. versicolor*, the Blue Flag, make imposing plants with their sword-like leaves. The only problem is the vigour of *I. pseudacorus* — it can get out of hand and cutting it back can be a tiresome

Iris pseudacorus 'Bastardi'

job. When pot-grown, the Yellow Flag reaches a height of 75 cm to 1 metre, while the Blue Flag is slightly smaller. Another yellow iris which is quite suitable for a pond of any size is *I. forrestii*, which grows to about 50 cm in height.

Another fine plant with yellow blooms, masses of them in fact, is *Cotula coronopifolia*. The common name is an appropriate one: Brass Buttons. This prostrate plant loves to spread over the surface of the water while producing scores of perfectly round bright yellow flowers. Brass Buttons must normally be treated as an annual, the seeds providing new plants the following year. Other summer flowering plants you might like to try are the Bog Arum, *Calla palustris*, with its white spathe and neat cordate leaves, growing about 25 cm high; the flowering rush *Butomus umbellatus*, which produces a spray of maroon flowers on top of what looks like the inverted frame of an umbrella; and the brilliantly coloured *Mimulus*, of which there are many varieties. By and large *Mimulus* prefer to be above water-level (*M. ringens*, with lavender flowers is an exception), but *M. luteus* (35 cm high) is often found growing in water in the wild. It is very similar to *M. guttatus*, which has a yellow flower blotched with red. *M.*

luteus lacks the blotches. Mimulus, or Monkey Flowers as they are often called, are very easy to grow and provide a fine show of colour. Raise your basket a little above the water line if necessary. A full basket will do much to conceal the rim. *Myosotis palustris* or Water Forget-me-not is an old favourite among water gardeners, and with good reason. Although the flowers are small, they are so daintily formed and of such an appealing shade of blue that they brighten any pond; and blue water plants, outside the tropics, are not common. For this reason, it is worth growing *Pontederia cordata*, the Pickerel Weed (45–75 cm) which, if it never flowered at all, would be worth having for its glossy, light green leaves, shaped like hearts. *P. cordata* flowers near the end of summer, after the Irises are over, as does the Water Mint, *Mentha aquatica*, which produces whorls of lilac. The height of this plant, with its green and bronzy leaves, is very variable. It may remain at 20 cm or may soar to more than twice that height. The Common Arrowhead – *Sagittaria sagittifolia* (50 cm high) with its characteristic arrow-shaped leaves, or the Japanese form *S. japonica* (75 cm), especially the double form which produces flowers like miniature snowballs – adds an unusual touch

Water Forget-Me-Not, Myosotis palustris.

Flowering Rush, Butomus umbellatus.

Prolific clumps of Cyperus longus, the Sweet Galingale, in a formal pond with water-lilies and iris.

to the pond. Take a visitor to the pond and those leaves always attract attention. Finally, among late summer- to autumn-flowering plants you might add one of the bulrushes with their brown poker flowers. (Actually the term bulrush strictly belongs to the genus *Scirpus* which does not have 'poker' flowers at all, but *Typha* are commonly also called bulrushes.) *Typha latifolia* is very vigorous and if you introduce it be sure to keep it within bounds. The smaller *T. angustifolia* can be kept within bounds when pot grown, but the obvious choice for the small pond is the little *T. minima*, which grows about 60 cm high.

Foliage plants will add a graceful touch to your pond, and those with variegated leaves add brightness and points of interest, especially when there may be nothing in flower. Sweet Galingale, *Cyperus longus*, has great arching leaves which are not only graceful but are excellent for flower arrangements. In a pot it should not exceed 75 cm in height, but be sure to cut off all shoots that break out of the pot or basket. *C. alternifolius* (best wintered indoors), known as the Umbrella Plant on account of the manner in which the leaves spread out in a circle above long stems, is most ornamental. It grows to much the same height as *C. longus*. An

exceptionally striking plant which well justifies its long name is *Scirpus tabernae-montani zebrinus*. Known as the Porcupine Quill Rush as well as the Zebra Rush, the plant has alternate green and cream bands ringing each stem (as well as sharp points at the end of each stem). Another variegated plant, and a most vivid one, is *Glyceria aquatica variegata*. While the *Scirpus* may exceed 1 metre in height, *Glyceria* (or Manna Grass) should not exceed 75 cm in a basket. Manna Grass is one of the most attractive plants that you can grow in a pond. Place a pot amongst irises or whatever, and see how it immediately breaks up the uniformity and monotony of greens. Another striking plant is *Acorus calamus variegatus*. Known as Sweet Flag, if you crush the leaves they will give off an aroma not unlike that of a tangerine orange. *Acorus calamus variegatus* grows to about 75 cm and produces a curious 'horn' for a flower, which emerges half way up the leaf. You might prefer the Japanese form, *A. gramineus variegatus*, which has two advantages. One is its size, it is only 30 cm high, and the other is very rare among water plants: it remains in character throughout the year.

Any list of marginal plants for a patio pond would have to include virtually every one of these plants. In contrast, as we shall see in the next chapter, it would be possible to draw up any number of lists of plants for the patio with little overlapping.

This pond, with cherub fountain, situated where two walls meet, provided with a canopy of climbing plants and heavily planted all around, epitomises a water feature which is both restful and tasteful.

9 Plants for the patio

The number of plants suitable for a patio is encyclopaedic, for the simple reason that virtually any plant that can be grown in a conventional garden can also be grown in or on a patio. Oak or beech, you might say, are hardly suitable for a patio, but even that is not quite true. The mighty beech, treated as a Bonsai plant, could find a place on the smallest patio. Faced with a choice that is well nigh unlimited, the best way of choosing your patio plants is to consider what kind of plants will be most useful. Straightaway, one can say that a certain number, if not all, should be evergreen. Most patios are used, at least occasionally, during winter and almost all are seen from the house, and the sight of nothing but skeleton boughs is not the most cheering. Another point to remember is that because evergreen trees shed their leaves continuously, in small numbers, they do not contribute to a major sweeping up operation in the autumn. Furthermore, deciduous leaves, if left in large numbers to become sodden on a patio, can become a real hazard. Wet leaves are very slippery.

Plants for the patio can be divided into roughly three categories: climbing plants, plants for gaps between paving slabs, and plants for tubs, terracotta pots and raised or flush beds. If your patio is already shaded and tending to be on the dark side, climbing plants may only make it feel more enclosed. Nothing is more suitable than a light-coloured wall whose reflection will greatly

Thymus drucei with its vivid purple flowers makes a lovely paving plant (see also the yellow Mimulus behind).

benefit adjacent plants. Where light is no problem, climbing plants are a decided asset in maturing and mellowing the whole area. Where you do not wish to go to the trouble of erecting a trellis, the obvious plant to choose is one of the many varieties of ivy (*Hedera*) which are self-clinging and evergreen. *Hedera helix* 'Goldheart', for example, will flourish in sun or shade. Moreover, it can be trained upwards or downwards, so covering the sides of raised beds if required. The Canary Island ivy, *H. canariensis* 'Variegata', has a much heavier leaf than the *helix* varieties and grows more rapidly. Ivy was once widely regarded as a symbol of love because it clings and embraces. According to Cornish legend, when Tristan and Iseult died, she of a broken heart, they were buried in the same graveyard, but the King ordered that they should be placed far apart. From each grave came forth a branch of ivy which met and intertwined as a remembrance of their love. In Greece a branch of ivy was given to newly-weds as a symbol of indissoluble wedlock.

No climber is more dramatic in appearance, especially in autumn, than the Virginian creeper, *Parthenocissus quinquefolia*, from North America, which will cover a wall very rapidly indeed, but does need attention if it is not to get out of hand. It can grow up to 20 m high, so this plant is best used only when a large-scale effect is needed. Remember too that it is deciduous. *P. henryana*, a Chinese form, has dark green leaves in summer turning to red in autumn, and grows up to about 10 m. Unlike the American form, however, this one is not fully hardy and needs a sheltered wall in Britain.

Where support can be provided, there is no more popular climbing plant than the innumerable varieties of *Clematis*. The *montana* varieties, which form hardwood stems, are very vigorous and will produce, without fail, a mass of flowers every spring. Hybrids such as the ever popular *C.* 'Nellie Moser', with pink and white striped flowers; 'Jackmanii superba', purple blue; and 'Ernest Markham', bright red, all flower through the summer months. For those who live in tropical or sub-tropical areas, even more vivid and exotic flowers are available with *Ipomoea* or Morning Glory. *I. purpurea* for example, a native of tropical America, produces trumpet flowers of the most vivid purple. The Mexican form, *I. coccinea*, has flowers of equally vivid red. These are vigorous climbers (which are usually regarded as annuals) with a height of about 3 m. The most exotic climber in temperate regions is surely the Passion Flower, *Passiflora caerulea*, which can attain a height of 10 m. Frost does, however, tend to take the top shoots off it, so grow on a sheltered wall. It has dark evergreen palmate leaves and strangely exotic purple and white flowers. There are a number of tender species, including *P. quadrangularis*, which produces edible fruits in favourable climates. The plant has been regarded as representing the mystical passion of Christ, hence the common name.

Hydrangea is not a plant commonly thought of as a climber and yet there are a number which are very suitable for a patio, including *Hydrangea petiolaris*, the Japanese climbing hydrangea, which is perfectly hardy and produces a mass of white flowers

Clematis 'Blue Diamond'

in June. If you want a winter-flowering climber you could hardly do better than choose *Jasminum nudiflorum*. Although it may attain a height of only 3 metres, this plant will thrive under almost any conditions. If you are wondering how to cover a sunless north wall then this plant is well worth trying. During the winter months it will produce small but bright yellow flowers. Finally in this category mention must be made of what to many is the finest of all climbing plants, the sweet-smelling Honeysuckle, which is available in both evergreen and deciduous forms, some hardy and some tender. *Lonicera periclymenum* is a British native and varieties of it are widely grown. It is deciduous. *L. japonica* has the advantage of being evergreen and is equally hardy. It is a vigorous plant easily attaining a height of 7 m or more.

Success in growing climbing plants depends primarily on good preparation of the soil. Dig down to a depth of at least 45 cm and a width of 60 cm. Use a good rich loam through which peat is mixed. If the loam contains a lot of clay and is liable to become water-logged, add sand. If available, enrich your soil with plenty of humus. It makes a great deal of difference.

Enriching the soil would be quite the wrong policy for most plants in the next category: prostrate and creeping plants suitable for the cracks and gaps between paving elements. Slabs laid on concrete and those laid without open joints are not, of course, suitable for planting. Paving plants are seen at their best amongst old natural flagstones, although they can sometimes be used effectively with concrete slabs. By leaving out whole patio slabs for the planting of low growing plants, geometric patterns can be made from plants and slabs. The reason why most paving plants should not be grown in rich soil is simply that it is unnatural to them. They grow too rapidly and can kill themselves in the process. My own favourite paving plant is *Thymus*, a plant which remains in character all the year round. I love the bright purple, white or lilac mounds of flowers that appear in late summer; and there is a particular pleasure in lying over or beside thyme in the heat of summer and taking in that characteristic fragrance. That is the attraction too of *Anthemis nobilis*, Common Chamomile, which has aromatic foliage and forms mossy carpets 15 to 20 cm high; and of *Mentha requienii*, which forms modest cushions only 2 to 3 cm high and has the smell of peppermint. Height is an important consideration if space is limited and you do not want the plants to appear too large and conspicuous. The best kind of paving plants, in my opinion, are those which one can walk over, such as thyme, chamomile and mint. Paving plants which are much higher may be awkward, especially for visitors who may wonder whether to walk round or over them, and may spend the entire evening fearing to tread on them! Hardier than *M. requienii*, which comes from Corsica, is the well-loved Pennyroyal, *Men-tha pulegium*, which was once used to ward off fleas and still has a use in the kitchen. It produces lilac flowers in later summer and requires a moister soil than most paving plants. *Aubretia deltoidea* is very popular for patios as it grows only about 10 cm high but spreads out very quickly. *Aubretia* is available in many bright colours as well, with white- and gold-edged leaves. The flowers appear in spring and continue well into the summer. The characteristic bell-shaped flowers of *Campanula* assure its popularity on the patio. Not all campanulas are hardy or small enough for gaps between pavings, but *C. pusilla (cochleariifolia)* is hardy, easily grown and does not exceed 12 cm in height. You can expect it to flower from mid summer until autumn. Again many colours are available, including pure white. For a mass effect of flowers stretching from spring to autumn one could combine with this campanula the Moss Phlox, *P. subulata*. Up to 10 cm high, varieties include the brilliant red 'Star Glow', a fine salmon pink called 'Alexander Surprise', and 'Bonita' which is a shade of blue, similar to lavender.

While paving plants are largely optional, it is how you fill your tubs and terracotta pots and beds that will contribute most to the character of your patio. Most gardeners, I think, aim at achieving a combination of

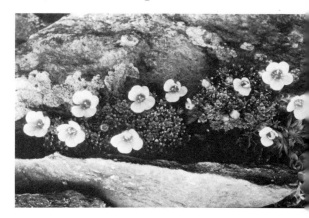

Saxifraga is an obliging plant that will thrive with little attention between the stones of paving or wall.

This is a garden with many elements: a round pond, gravel surround and brick patio, concrete dais, potted geraniums and fuchsia. Yet they all combine to produce a calm atmosphere because each element is itself gentle and unobtrusive.

those shrubs which are grown for their brilliant blossom and those which are attractive mainly on account of their foliage. Foliage plants deserve priority, for foliage is what softens and enlivens building materials and which will create in your patio a sense of repose. To keep your patio in character through the year most of the shrubs should be evergreen. A plant which combines all these virtues of fine foliage, conspicuous white flowers and being evergreen is *Fatsia japonica*. The leaves are like huge, glossy green fingers. *Fatsia* flowers in October and does well in a tub, growing to about 3 m. In urban areas few plants are as popular as *Fatsia*. Try to protect from severe frosts which may damage those spectacular leaves. Another evergreen with glossy, if plain, leaves is the *Camellia*. The characteristic vivid blooms are available in many shades of red and pink as well as white. One is probably better off choosing the single or semi-double varieties, as the double forms sometimes drop their buds before opening. Camellias need acid soil to which has been added plenty of peat, and are

therefore particularly suitable for tubs and pots. They do not like too much direct sunshine and do best in a shady, protected corner. Frost can easily nip the bud and blossom. In summer the roots should be kept cool, and thereupon depends much of the success of this lovely plant. The blooms of rhododendrons and azaleas (they belong to the same genus) are just as brilliant as those of camellias, and the smaller azaleas are very suitable for pot culture. There are many evergreen forms. Again the soil must be acid and the addition of peat and leaf mould is very beneficial. Never allow the soil to dry out, that can be fatal; on the other hand the soil should not remain water-logged. Semi-shade and a sheltered spot is ideal. *R. praecox* will provide you with pink to purple trumpet flowers at the very beginning of spring. It grows to about 1 m or a little more in height. By comparison, *R. ponticum* grows only about 45 cm tall. As *R. praecox* drops its blooms, *R. ponticum* will burst forth in April and May, producing bright blue flowers. Later again come two of the most brilliant azaleas, *A.*

'Hinodegiri', which has bright red flowers, and *A.* 'Hinomayo' with light pink. They form an excellent combination. By judicious selection of camellias, rhododendrons and azaleas it is possible to have blooms extending through many months (individually they have a rather short season). Fuchsias, on the other hand, flower over a period of months; and to have a display of their pendulous 'ballerina' flowers is one of the great delights of patio gardening. Fuchsias must be among the most widely grown of tub and pot plants. Some are tender, but there is no problem about having them outdoors during the summer provided they are kept well watered. A clever subterfuge is simply to bury the pot or container in your raised bed in early summer and lift again in autumn for wintering indoors. *Fuchsia* 'Swingtime' is a fine example of the innumerable varieties now grown, the flower consisting of bright red 'bodice' with a double skirt of white. The pendulous habit makes this fuchsia suitable for hanging over the edge of a trough or pot. *F.* 'Alice Hoffman' is somewhat similar and can be wintered outdoors, as can *F.* 'Mission Bells' which has red and purple flowers. Grown in pots these fuchsias are not likely to exceed 1m in height.

For their spreading, elegant form as well as for the brilliance of their flowers, magnolias can contribute a great deal to a patio area. Only *M. grandiflora* is evergreen, however, and this tree can reach a height of 5m. It is best grown against a wall. For the small patio *M. stellata* is the obvious choice, producing star-shaped flowers in early spring. It is a dwarf of the species, reaching about 2m in height in a large tub. If you want to fill a corner with a dense, bushy shrub, then you might choose *Hydrangea macrophylla serrata* whose spread is about equal to its height of 1.5m. It is in flower from mid summer until autumn. The pink and white forms of *H. macrophylla* can be grown in any soil, but the blue forms require soil that is thoroughly acidic if the tones are to achieve their maximum density. Hydrangeas appreciate soil that contains plenty of manure. Rather the opposite, poor soil is what satisfies the rock rose, *Cistus*, along with plenty of sun away from east winds. These plants do not transplant easily, so buy only pot-grown specimens. No shrub gives better value in terms of colour during the summer. Day after day, the wonderful tissue paper-thin blooms open and close the same day, never to open again. But so profuse is the Rock Rose that a succession of blooms continues unremittingly for the whole season. A *Cistus* in bloom — those papery petals and silvery grey leaves swaying gently in a breeze — is a pleasure almost unique to that plant (sweeping up of petals dropped daily is the only drawback). *C. ladaniferus*, which can reach 2m, has white flowers blotched with maroon. *C. purpureus* is a little smaller and has pink to purple flowers, while *C.* 'Silver pink' has pink flowers and a height and spread of only 1m.

Terracotta pots have been in use since time immemorial and always impart a sense of age to a patio. Japanese maples look well in almost any kind of container, but the sense of serenity that their spreading branches offer seems to be particularly well suited to terracotta pots. *Acer palmatum dissectum viridis*

Magnolia stellata

produces brilliant light green leaves in spring that turn to orange of equal brilliance in autumn. The purple form, *A. palmatum dissectum purpureum*, is equally suitable for pot culture. Both are extremely slow growing plants, so a height of 1.5 m would only be reached after many years. More noticeable than their gain in height is the manner in which the boughs gain in spread. Harsh, frost-laden winds can easily damage the leaf, otherwise maples are trouble free.

If you have a barbecue, *Laurus nobilis*, the Sweet Bay, is an excellent choice. In sun or shade the Bay will thrive. Grown in a pot, the Sweet Bay is not likely to much exceed 2 m. The flowers are inconspicuous, but the leaves are a lovely shade of darkest green. Pluck them to season your meat or fish. Try adding a leaf or two directly to the charcoal. Being evergreen, the Sweet Bay is ready for use at any time.

Another genus that should be considered for any patio scheme is *Juniperus*. All species of juniper are evergreen and their great variety of form gives them a wide application. *J. scopulorum* 'Skyrocket', compact and columnar, will, for example, give a flat area a welcome sense of height. A good height for a pot-grown specimen is 2 m. *Juniperus* x *media* 'Pfitzeriana' has a low spreading habit suitable for a space in the patio floor. *J. sabina tamariscifolia* is similar but has the additional attraction of layered branches. You need a free space of 1.5 m to grow these spreading plants, but nothing perhaps compares with junipers in giving a patio a sense of having matured.

But a selection of any of these plants, used with discrimination, will mature the patio without overcrowding it. They will help to turn what is initially a building area into a garden. For those who wish to grow bedding plants, there should still be room to grow Pelargoniums (geraniums) — perhaps the most popular patio and tub plant of all — begonias, *Tropaeolum* and bulbs. Pelargoniums are readily grown from cuttings taken in late summer and put out the following spring. The nasturtium *Tropaeolum polyphyllum*, with its yellow flowers, is perennial and suitable for trailing in a dry area. It has a spread of between 1 and 2 m. The small annual forms, such as 'Jewel Mixed' (semi-double in yellow and shades of pink and red) are readily grown from seed. They make a great show in a limited space, only growing about 35 cm high.

Finally you might consider the most natural of all kinds of walls: a hedge. It has many advantages. A hedge often provides better wind shelter than a solid wall, simply because it is not solid. Wind meeting a solid obstruction may actually gather speed in passing over it, with the surprising result that turbulence is created on the leeward side. Most hedging plants are cheap by comparison with man-made materials, and a hedge can be put in without difficulty after the patio is laid. If you have difficulty in opting for one kind of hedge as opposed to another, try the process of elimination. Let us say you want your hedge to grow only 90 or 140 cm high. Then that should be sufficient reason for you to resist the temptation of buying a fast growing hedge. *Chamaecyparis lawsoniana* and more especially *Cupressocyparis leylandii* can grow at an astonishing speed. They are ideal for large windbreaks; but you would never have done with trimming them if you wanted a small hedge. They are suitable only if you want a tall hedge in the shortest possible time. If you want to use or even view your patio out of the summer months, it will not be much fun staring at a hedge that has become a skeleton after the autumn. That means you can exclude all deciduous trees. An exception you might feel could be made for *Fagus sylvatica* (the Common Beech) whose gorgeous bright green leaves turn to russet in autumn and remain on the bough through the winter. As against that it is strenuous work cutting back beech. That might not be much of a factor if the patio is small, but think of the continual dropping of leaves over many months. You would always be sweeping them up. Another point is the rustling of dead beech leaves on the bough. Take a walk through an autumnal or wintry beech wood and that sound can be exhilarating. At close quarters over many months you might find it too much.

A popular garden shrub is *Berberis darwinii* with its bright berries. It makes a dense hedge which few animals can penetrate. As against that its thorns are troublesome when cutting back, and on a small patio extending branches can cause nasty scratches. There are no such problems with *Escallonia macrantha*, with its lovely red flowers, or the beautiful vivid pink *E.* 'Apple Blossom'. They like a mild climate (they are excellent for coastal areas) and should not be trimmed back too hard if they are to flower well. Another shrub particularly well suited to coastal areas is *Griselinia littoralis*. The popularity of this shrub does, I suppose, prove its worth. It is dense, compact and reliable, and cheap to buy. But I would be reluctant to surround my patio with it; its bright, broad leaves strike me as being overbearing. One might feel too enclosed by *Griselinia*, which needs space. On the other hand I would not shun the common privet, *Ligustrum ovalifolium*, perhaps the cheapest of all hedging plants. You might regard privets as too common and inconspicuous; perhaps they are over-used but their very inconspicuousness I would regard as a virtue, not a vice. Your hedge should form a backdrop to the main source of interest: the patio, tub plants and pond. *Ceanothus* 'Southmead', for example, has small leaves and is of compact habit. *Ceanothus* (there are deciduous varieties and evergreens) forms a beautifully quiet background to almost anything you might think of putting on the patio. At the same time it has its moment of glory when those distinctive light or rich dark blue flowers burst forth. Obviously maintaining *Ceanothus*

in a good shape will reduce its flowers, but it does make a neat hedge.

For a truly formal hedge I would choose *Taxus baccata*, Common Yew, for it can be clipped to geometric perfection. So too can *Buxus sempervirens*, Common Box, which our forefathers used so well. (*Buxus* is less vigorous than the widely grown *Lonicera nitida* but is very similar in appearance. Choose Box and you make a considerable saving on labour.) At the other extreme, if you want a casual, billowy hedge you might choose *Rosmarinus officinalis*, Rosemary, or *Lavandula spica (officinalis)*. The blue flowers of Rosemary are lovely and lasting, and plucking the leaves for their aroma (and using them on your barbecue) all adds to the enjoyment of your patio. Old English Lavender has long silver-grey leaves and bluish flowers, and grows only a metre and a half, if that. There is indeed much to be said for a hedge.

Dig over the ground thoroughly before planting. Plant the hedge using a builder's line and space evenly. Slow-growing shrubs should be spaced at intervals of between 30 and 45 cm, the faster ones at up to 60 cm. A top mulch of manure will help to keep the area weed free. But for about two years after planting, care must be taken to make sure the line of the hedge is not encroached upon by grass or weeds. Stake the plants if necessary and after high winds make sure the roots have not been loosened. Re-firm with your feet as necessary. Keep the hedge watered until established. When trimming your hedge, creating a slightly triangular appearance will ensure that the bottom of the hedge gets light. In this way the foliage should remain evenly distributed from top to bottom.

We have now considered the construction of both pond and patio, and how they might both be planted. Another dimension altogether is possible with the introduction of fish and livestock into the pond, the subject of the next chapter.

Koi, Shubunkin and other goldfish displaying their splendid colours.

10 Fish for the patio pond

To watch fish wending their way silently through the undergrowth of water plants, or rising to the surface to collect a titbit, to see them mating in spring and watch the growth of fish young and old, is one of the pleasures of pond keeping. Fish become tame with time. Learning to associate your appearance with food, they will follow you round the pond, endlessly circling the area near to you in expectation of being fed. Some fish, if one invests a little time and patience, may even take food from your fingers. If you have ever kept fish in a pond, you probably find that you automatically seek them out in any pond you visit; and a pond without fish, no matter how fine the array of plants, somehow seems incomplete. I can think of only one disadvantage in keeping fish. Some fish spend more time than others feeding on the surface, but all fish, from time to time, will grub round the bottom of the pool sending up little clouds of mud. As a result, a fish pond will not have quite the same clarity as one from which fish are absent. But this is a small point. A pond that is on the deep side rather than on the shallow side will, obviously, be less affected by the activity of fish grubbing round for food. In any case the advantages of keeping fish far outweigh this minor consideration. Fish not only have an ornamental value, they also assist in keeping down many pests.

Before introducing fish into your pond, allow the water, if drawn from a tap, to settle for a few days. This will enable the chlorine in the water to evaporate. Even better, first allow your underwater plants to start growing and to develop roots. Fish tend to uproot oxygenating plants which are not firmly established. As regards the 'pea soup' stage that the water must inevitably go through, when the growth of algae far outstrips the growth of the oxygenators, fish will thrive in this condition. Unhealthy as the water may look at this stage, it is in fact more suitable for fish than newly introduced water which may contain harmful chemicals. Water rich in algae is healthy water and the fish will happily feed off the tiny organisms.

If you have used concrete or mortar in any part of the construction of the pond, make quite sure that lime has not found its way into the water. If it has, rinse the pond out well before introducing fish. A liner pond would appear to offer no such danger. But if it is a raised pond, what about the coping? Lime can leach from the joints, and the coping itself might contain lime. Another danger, easily overlooked, is the use of new concrete blocks to support marginal plants, where a shelf has not been built into the pond. Several such blocks in a small space can easily raise the lime in the pond to a level that fish cannot tolerate. If you have coping round your pond or have bought concrete blocks to use as supports, allow the materials to weather in rain for at least several weeks. Otherwise, use a patent sealer to 'cure' the concrete. The best guide as to when fish may be safely introduced is to see the underwater plants in active growth, light green buds emerging from darker foliage.

When you buy your fish make sure that they are healthy specimens. If you have any doubts about the health of the fish and fear infecting fish that you already have in the pond, you could quarantine the newcomers. This can be done by keeping them for a few weeks in another pond or an indoor tank. Any reputable dealer will have quarantined his stock before putting them up for sale. But fish, like all other living creatures, are still liable to a variety of ills, so choose your stock with care. Fish which are in good condition should exhibit liveliness. When you approach the tank they should scurry away at speed. Fish which are ill, not surprisingly, exhibit the opposite characteristics. They appear listless, as opposed to merely moving slowly. If they do not swim perfectly upright with deft movement, then do not buy them. Also take note of the dorsal fin, that is the fin directly in the middle of the back; if the dorsal fin is not erect then the fish may not be in the best of health. In fish which have highly developed dorsal fins, you will notice that the motion of the water gives these fins a billowy effect. This is normal and attractive. By contrast, a fish out of condition will have a dorsal fin that seems floppy rather than billowy. In a nutshell, select fish which are lively and energetic.

An important point to remember is not to transfer fish from one temperature to another without giving them time to adjust. Cold water fish can adapt to extremes of temperature but they cannot do so instantaneously. Most fish are conveniently transported in polythene bags. When you arrive at your pond, open the neck of the bag, and allow the bag to float on the pond. The temperature of the water in the bag will gradually become the same as the pond temperature. Then simply tip the bag over and allow the fish to escape into the pond.

They usually rush off to hide themselves in weeds or rocks. (Always make sure that fish have protection from direct sunlight, which they can use as they wish.) After a little time they will emerge to explore their new surroundings, wending their way round the pond only to dash off at the slightest sight of their new owner. However, they will soon become accustomed to you and will look forward, with eager swirling movements, to being fed on your arrival.

The common goldfish (*Carassius auratus*) still remains the most popular choice for the garden pool, and with good reason. It is an adaptable fish, very conspicuous, hardy in most climates and making do with small quarters if needs be. Most important of all, its oxygen needs are satisfied by the natural absorption of oxygen by the water from the surrounding air. It is unwise, nevertheless, to overstock your pond. That is a common cause of disease and, besides, a crowded pond is unaesthetic. Advice differs as to the number of fish a pond of a particular size can support. The relevant consideration is the surface area of water (because it is the surface through which oxygen is absorbed), rather

Allow the polythene bag in which your fish have been transported to rest for an hour or more on the surface of the pond. The neck of the bag should be opened. The object is to allow the water in the bag to gradually adjust to the temperature in the pond.

than the depth. So far as goldfish are concerned, a square metre of water could support at least three fish, but two would look better. The common goldfish is a descendant of the dark European Crucian Carp (*Carassius carassius*) and now many hundreds of varieties are available. There is, for example, the Comet Goldfish, whose tail fins measure about a third of the length of the entire body; while the so-called Fantail Goldfish has a short and very rotund body in addition to a very conspicuous, deep, flowing tail. The Black Moor is very similar to the Fantail, except it has large bulbous (known as telescopic) eyes, and, as the name would suggest, is entirely black save for the silvery belly. Generally speaking, the more symmetrical the finnage on these exotic – and grotesque – forms, the more expensive they become; and one can pay fancy prices. However, the finer points of symmetry can really be observed only at close quarters in an aquarium and so are rather wasted in a patio pond. Besides, symmetry has no bearing on the health of an individual fish.

Gold and yellow are by no means the only colours available in the genus *Carassius*. Shubunkins are highly mottled, most commonly in combinations of blue, black, white and red. They appear to be scaleless on account of the fact that their colour pigment is not contained in the scales. Blue Shubunkins are the most highly prized, and in the best forms, such as Cambridge Blue Shubunkins, blue predominates over the other colours on the fish. Shubunkins are available in a variety of forms as well as colour, and are as hardy as goldfish.

Goldfish serve a useful purpose in eating aphids and other unwanted pests. But there is another fish which fulfils this role even more efficiently. This is the Golden Orfe (*Idus idus*) which is the favourite fish of many pond-lovers. Longer and more slender than the common goldfish, it spends more time near the surface of the pond and moves about with a rapid, darting motion. Young Orfe

The Black Moor

often travel in shoals. There is a satisfying contrast to be had in keeping both goldfish and Golden Orfe. The more peaceful, gentle movement of the goldfish contrasts with the vivacious dash of the Orfe. While gold is the most usual colour for Orfe, occasionally one can find a silver form. Orfe are perfectly hardy, although they require more space than goldfish and are most unlikely to breed in a patio pond.

In spring when the water temperature rises to between 15° and 18°C, you may see a series of small dots developing on the gill plates of some cock goldfish. This is an indication that breeding is likely to ensue. The cock fish frantically chase the hen fish round and round the pond, until the eggs are deposited and fertilized. This usually takes place on weed and in shallow water if such is available. In five days or less, the minute, translucent young hatch. As fish are notorious cannibals, it is a distinct advantage to remove all adult fish to another pond or tank at this stage. Goldfish have the tendency to revert to the black or brown colour of their ancestors. Any batch of fish that you raise is likely to contain reversions, but remember that fry and young fish which are dark in colour may well turn to yellow or gold with time.

Goldfish, Shubunkins and Golden Orfe should be the first choice for the patio pond.

Golden Rudd (*Scardinius erythrophthalmus aurata*) is not unlike the Golden Orfe in appearance, although its colouring is less bright, and it does make a suitable pond fish. Green and Golden Tench (*Tinca tinca/aurata*) have a reputation for scavenging around the bottom of the pond, performing a useful cleaning-up operation. Their use in this regard is exaggerated, and because they tend to stay at the bottom of the pool, well away from the light, they are rarely seen. Koi and Higoi Carp are easily the most brilliant of all pond fish. They have large appetites and readily take food from the hand, but also love grubbing round in the bottom of the pond and tend to uproot oxygenators and even water-lilies. They also like plenty of space and a high oxygen content in the water. But whatever you decide about Koi Carp, never introduce the Common Perch (*Perca fluviatilis*) or Catfish (*Ictalurus nebulosos*) into an ornamental pond containing other fish. They are predators and will eat their unfortunate companions who are forced to share the same environs.

A pond that is well stocked with underwater plants, sufficient to keep the water clear, should also provide sufficient food, both in terms of foliage and insect life, for your fish without additional feeding. Keep your stock of food for when you want to encourage the fish to come to the surface or to get used to your presence. Variety of diet is all to the good. Fish flakes, *Daphnia*, tiny earthworms, chopped up if you do not regard that as unbearable, and even well chopped up hard-boiled egg. Actually, the boiled egg should be mashed up rather than chopped up; and as it can very easily pollute the pond, provide no more than is quickly eaten by the fish. In autumn, extra feeding can be given to build the fish up for winter.

The question as to whether fish can survive in a pond during frost and particularly ice is often asked. The answer is that the common goldfish (as opposed to the squat-bodied forms, which are delicate), Golden Orfe and the other species mentioned, can all adapt to extremes of temperature and even to a covering of ice on the pond. It is not the ice itself which constitutes a danger but the fact that a sheet of ice remaining on a pond for a sustained period traps in the water noxious gases which would normally escape into the air. This can be fatal to fish, especially if there has been a build-up of leaves in the pond during the autumn. Leaves are a major source of pond pollution. Pond water should never turn blackish or greyish, nor should the surface ever have an oily sheen. These are all indications of pollution. One way of dealing with the problem of ice is to install a pond heater. The object of this device is to keep a small hole open in the ice. It can make the difference between life and death for the fish. A pond heater merely prevents the ice forming in a small area; it does not, nor need to, melt the ice over the entire pond. As it uses only about 150 watts, running costs are not high. On no account crack or otherwise break up the ice to achieve the same purpose. Fish are highly sensitive to vibration and the cracking of ice can injure them fatally. In the absence of a pond heater, if you want to make a hole in the ice, use hot or boiling water from a kettle.

Fish, more especially small fish and fry, have a number of natural enemies. These include the Water Scorpion (*Nepa cinerea*), the Water Boatman (*Notonecta glauca*) and dragonfly larvae, which will prey on fish if they are very small. I feel that one cannot deal with every insect that finds its way to the pond, that young fish must take their chance in the natural order of things; and besides, insects add to the richness of pond life. An exception might be made in the case of the fearsome *Dystiscus marginalis* or Great Diving Beetle. It is easily identified by its size (30 to 35 mm long) and its shiny black body which has lighter, usually brownish, markings and legs. Smaller beetles of the same genus are less troublesome, and cannot be confused with their large cousin because beetles do not

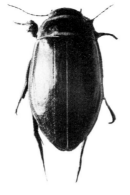

Pond pests. Left: the Water Boatman, Notonecta glauca; middle: the Great Diving Beetle, Dystiscus marginalis right: the Water Scorpion, Nepa cinerea.

grow in size after the pupa stage, from which they emerge fully grown. The Great Diving Beetle is quite capable of attacking fish larger than itself. As it has to surface periodically to take in air, you should be able to net this beetle.

As regards other livestock for the pond, water snails are often looked upon as an important factor in keeping the water clean. In fact their effect on algal growth is insignificant; and some snails will devour the leaves of *Nymphaea*, the miniature varieties in particular, as well as some floating plants. The Great Pond Snail, *Limnaea stagnalis*, is the culprit. It can be recognised by its pointed, conical shell up to 50 mm high. If a single specimen gets into your pond, be it male or female, it can still reproduce. It is an hermaphrodite and is capable of fertilizing its own eggs. Even if you pick off these snails from plants that you introduce into your pond, their eggs laid in strings of jelly and adhering to plants tend to find their way in.

However, these snails really become a serious pest only in the case of miniature water-lilies, which can succumb to their feeding habits. If you want to introduce snails into your pond, then obtain the Great Ramshorn Snail, *Planorbis corneus*, which is about 35 mm wide, conical but not pointed. This snail is far less hardy, however, and may not take to the conditions in your pond. You can but introduce a few and see how they fare.

Amphibians, frogs, toads and newts are loathed by some, welcomed by others. I personally look forward to the throng of frogs that visit the ponds round about every spring and hide among the undergrowth or play on the lawn on wet nights. I only wish newts were as common. But in any case none of these lovely creatures is suitable for the patio pond unless there is a large garden besides with an abundance of greenery. The patio pond is not their natural habitat.

We have now covered the construction of both pond and patio, and considered how both might be stocked. One question remains: how all these components can best be combined — in other words the question of design.

Pond snails of the genus Planorbis (left) and Limnaea (right).

11 The question of design

Is it possible to write usefully about designing a garden? I suspect the majority of readers may be sceptical. Design, it will be argued, is assimilated not taught, certainly not in books. Practical advice on construction is one thing, taste is quite another. There is a certain amount of truth in this view, but it is not the whole truth. Design is not simply a matter of taste. It is also a question of dealing with practical considerations; and the more carefully planned the patio and pond before construction is begun, the more successful is likely to be the result. The design of any patio scheme, of whatever kind, must involve certain basic considerations.

How big should the patio be?

None is more basic than determining that the patio is large enough for your needs. To suggest that the patio must be large enough to accommodate chairs, to be walked upon without awkward obstructions such as shrubs (especially wet with rain) catching your clothes, or the sharp corner of a raised pond catching your ankle, may seem too obvious. Yet these points are often overlooked. Make the free space in your patio too small and

The shape of a pond can be a critical factor in design. To test this, cover the right-hand section of this zig-zag pond with one hand and notice how plain the pond in the foreground suddenly becomes. The fact that the pond consists of two long rectangles joined by a smaller section adds a great deal to the overall design.

your design is wrong from the start. Four chairs and a small occasional table require a free space of not less than 2.2×2.6 m. You can determine this for yourself by experiment. Four people can certainly be seated round a coffee table in a more confined space, but inevitably, given a little time, everyone wants to stretch their legs, change the angle of their chairs, turn to face the sun. A larger space is desirable if it can be accommodated. I suggest you first decide upon how much free space you require and make all else of a size to comply with it. Remember that the pond or fountain, the pond especially, can hardly be too small. All too easily, in an excess of enthusiasm, a pond is made too large. Nothing destroys the sense of proportion in a patio more than the feeling of being swamped by a pond, of walking gingerly around its perimeter, taking careful steps around corners that seem to encroach on the patio. As a rule of thumb the length and width of a pond should not exceed a third of the width and length of the patio. More often it should be much less. The width of the patio between a wall and the pond, so far as walking in comfort is concerned, should be about 1 metre, and rather more should be allowed for a hedge (even a mature one) whose width will, of course, vary. Much less than a metre and one has the feeling of being hemmed in.

The question of where to site the free space, and where the pond, is an important one and often a compromise has to be

Fig. 38. In tropical and sub-tropical climates the flowers of marginal plants in a pond may suffer from too much direct sunlight. Under such conditions the dappled shade provided by louvres can be an advantage.

reached. This at least is likely to be the case in Britain where sunshine is at a premium. If your patio is equally exposed to the sun at all points then the free space and the pond can really be sited where you wish. However, if shadows are cast across the area for long periods, one should bear in mind that water-lilies need direct sunlight for at least half the day to flower well. In Scotland this would be too little. The potential of *Nymphaea* to flower is in direct proportion to the amount of sun they receive. If your patio is shaded for long periods or is entirely in shade, it would be as well to emphasise the pleasure of water in motion and do without *Nymphaea* and water plants. In places such as California and Florida, partial shade may be regarded as desirable for both occupants and certain water plants, such as irises, whose flowers may fade and go over more quickly in direct sunshine. The important thing is to be well aware of the importance of free open space in the patio and how it will be affected by shadows cast by high walls. Where shadow is a major problem the painting of your walls with white or a light coloured paint can brighten up the area to a surprising extent. A heavy covering of ivy (*Hedera*) or other climbing plants will, of course, have the opposite effect.

Talking of plants, it is worth mentioning the drawback of planting shrubs directly in spaces left in the patio. Delay this at least until the patio has had some use. Just as rabbits and badgers develop certain well worn tracks, so you will find your family will use the patio in a particular way. Certain routes are found more convenient than others and become established. For this reason I am reluctant to incorporate directly planted shrubs in the original scheme. They can often turn out to be in just the wrong place.

Shape and size for the pond or fountain

Having satisfied yourself that you have located your free space in the right place and it is of sufficient size (do remember if the space looks bare it can be added to at any time with tubs and pots), then go on to decide the dimensions of your pond or fountain. So far as a fountain is concerned the main consideration is that it does not overwhelm the patio. The dimensions are not the only

Several features of this patio pond are noteworthy. The fountain urn and the pond are in exactly the right proportion to each other. The paving used around the pond contrasts with the brick patio and so emphasises the pond. The surrounding shrubs remove any harshness that the building materials might suggest on their own.

factors involved here; its bulk, shape, texture and colour all contribute to the impact of the sculpture. The eye is the best guide in this instance, and guidelines are hard to provide. If in doubt choose a smaller rather than a larger fountain. The criticism that a sculpture is too small is heard far less frequently than that a sculpture is too large. Where your patio is surrounded by high walls, the space can usually take a larger fountain to balance the enclosing effect of the walls. On the other hand if you have a very low hedge or wall, say only 60 or 90 cm in height, then a high fountain may look ungainly – protruding from its surroundings in an uncomfortable way.

Fig. 39. Often enough one is confronted with a dark corner to fill. Water plants are unlikely to thrive. A formal waterfall, be it in one or more tiers, will always make a strong feature.

In almost every case, a formal pond is more suitable for a patio than a so-called free-form or informal one. There are exceptions: when the patio is bounded by an irregular, twisting hedge (especially when composed of mixed shrubs) *and* when the patio material is made up of crazy paving or irregular slabs. A free-form pool is virtually impossible to combine successfully with interlocking or formal paving slabs. The geometry of the formal is nearly always in opposition to the free flowing irregular lines of the pond. An exception is shown in the photograph below, where the brief was to use square red tiles (surplus to another job) with an informal pond and a rockery. The resulting design involved two critical features. In the first place, a decision was taken that only part of the perimeter of the pond would be met by tiles. The aim was to create the impression of the informal meeting the formal, rather than one being encompassed by the other. Secondly, the hard edge of the tiles was deliberately softened by laying them in a vaguely circular manner; and thirdly, the hard edge was partly obscured by the use of prostrate plants. Take a look at the photograph. If you feel the two sections, the informal pond and the rockery on the one hand, the patio and barbecue on the other, occupy two independent but related territories, then the design has succeeded. If you feel there is still a conflict between formal and informal then the design has failed.

Regular, formal ponds are best made in simple shapes. Try to design your pond so that the patio slabs can be easily fitted round it. Polygonal ponds require extremely accurate cutting of paving elements. To cut a triangular piece for an inconspicuous corner offers little difficulty. Cutting perhaps six or eight such pieces so that they provide an absolutely symmetrical border to a pond is

An unusual design concept: an attempt to have the formal, represented by the tile patio, interlock with an irregular pond and natural rockery.

exceedingly difficult. Where possible, use the uncut edge of the paving slab to face the pond. If the cut edge is in any way rough or uneven, placing it adjacent to another slab will minimise such defects. The cutting round the base of a raised pond need not, of course, be quite so accurate, as the paving slabs will not be required to create a smooth brink.

There are supposed to be ideal dimensions for a rectangular pond. In the time of classical Greece, Pythagoras propounded a theory of proportion. Now known as Kepler's 'Golden Measure' it suggests that the ratio of the length of a rectangle to its side should be 1.618:1. How that measurement is obtained is shown in the figure. It is unlikely that exactly those proportions would suit your specific situation, but the ratio is not purely academic. As a matter of interest compare the ratio you have obtained with the Greek model. If the length of your pond is in a greater ratio to the width, then your pond will appear elongated. If the ratio is smaller, then your pond may appear stubby. At all costs avoid a square pond: no other shape is quite so unappealing. There is a deadness about a square shape. Be bold in your proportions but not extreme.

Nothing is more important than that the lines of your pond should run parallel with the boundary lines of the patio. Ponds that are off square are irritating and the soothing effect of water and lilies is inevitably compromised. Lines that are not parallel must be made very strong and obvious to avoid any suggestion that the pond is not simply askew. It is a risky business. A feature can be made of a pond placed, for example, diagonally across the patio. There is a danger, however, in going against the grain, as unusual lines tend to distract rather than to guide the eye to and along harmonious lines.

Very often the dimensions of the patio area are pre-determined by existing walls. If your patio is long and narrow, a rectangular pond running lengthwise will emphasise the nar-

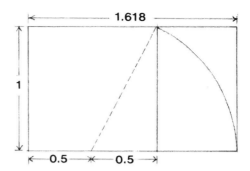

Fig. 40. Kepler's Golden Measure.

rowness of the area. On the other hand a pond placed crosswise will make the patio look somewhat broader. There is a catch, however. A *single* item running crosswise gives the impression of a conflict of lines: the long ones of the boundary walls set at right angles to the pond. Since the boundary lines are the dominant ones, the pond may look a little like an obstruction to them. So if you have one element going against the grain, then you must have another. Two or three items forming cross rhythms comprise a feature in their own right and cease to be a single, contrary exception to the 'grain'. Parallel with the pond you could place a seat, a raised or flush bed or several tubs forming a geometric group. If your patio appears too broad, a far less common complaint, then the opposite remedy will solve that problem. Place the pond, tubs and beds lengthwise to make the area appear less broad.

The illusion of space

As garden space continues to shrink, one of the greatest challenges of modern design is to create the illusion of greater size. It is a challenge which draws upon all the experience and skill that the designer can muster. Whatever the final design for any small space, two underlying principles will have been used. The first is simple enough: variety increases the sense of space, presumably because unconsciously we react by associating multiplicity with size, i.e. the more objects perceived the greater must be the space to enclose them. The danger is making the patio too cluttered. Variety is only useful if adequate space is left between the various items, tubs, raised borders, terracotta pots or whatever. The sense of spaciousness will only be achieved if this requirement is recognised. Furthermore, the various items should not be situated in random order but should form clusters or groups. This leads to the second and perhaps more important principle for achieving a sense of spaciousness. That is to treat the patio area not as a single unit but as two or more areas, in such a way that the whole patio cannot be taken in from a single glance or a single vantage point. For example, a feature made in a corner, a statue, fountain or pond, could be partially obscured by a large shrub or tree, or trellis work or brickwork. It is quite extraordinary how much atmosphere, in addition to spaciousness, partitioning achieves. The partition must not be total, indeed to block off one area from another is to defeat the purpose of the exercise. The aim should be to indicate, to partially reveal, the existence of another area within the patio which can only be explored by moving from one place to another. Therein lies the real secret of enlarging a small space.

The split-level patio

There is one feature, perhaps above all others, which can add immeasurably to a patio. That is to divide the area into two or more different heights – split-level, in other words. Quite why this should be so effective is not easy to say. There may be more than one reason. It may have something to do with the way we perceive a given area. The eye quickly takes in a flat area. It is bland as compared with a split-level. Somehow, whatever else may be contained in or on the patio, the very fact that it is of varying heights intensifies the level of interest.

In starting a patio from scratch, I would always consider whether it is feasible to turn the area into two or more levels. Very often a backyard is left with a sizeable heap of rubble, especially if an extension has been added to the house. The effort of carting the stuff to a refuse skip, perhaps some distance off, often deters the owner from clearing it at all. Nothing is more suitable nor more convenient for making a split-level patio. If the raised area is carefully calculated it can be made with the rubble available without discarding any of it nor importing more. The rubble, thoroughly compacted, must be contained with brick or block courses.

Raised beds and ponds

Mention has already been made of the fact that water-lilies and plants can be accommodated in the smallest of ponds. Where raised ponds are concerned, the thickness of the walls must be taken into account. The water will seem a very insignificant feature if the interior measurements of the walls are only slightly greater than the thickness of the walls. As a guide, do not make the internal width of the pond less than three times the thickness of the wall. Another point to remember with raised ponds is to make them a conspicuous height above the patio (this is even more important if the raised pond and patio are made of the same material). A single course of bricks jutting out of the patio is most unsatisfactory. Is it a raised pond or simply a coping that has not been laid flush with the surrounding slabs? Make a raised pond with at least several courses. A raised pond can provide a good flat surface for sitting upon – and observing pond life – and a suitable height is around 600 mm (2 feet). Raised ponds will provide an additional sense of solidity to the patio area, though

A brilliant patio design, not only on account of the hexagonal motif, displayed both horizontally and vertically, but also for the manner in which an uncomfortably narrow garden is made to look broader.

A Japanese pot-grown Maple makes a fine patio feature. In this instance its importance on the patio is endorsed by having a special inlay in the paving.

constructed between doors and patio. Raised beds are not only an asset to the disabled but to the elderly and those whose backs give trouble (and whose back does not give trouble from time to time?). Weeding a border while sitting on a brick surround, especially on a sunny morning, makes weeding a far less onerous chore. Besides, raised beds designed in a variety of shapes make an attractive feature in their own right.

their bulky effect may need to be balanced by other features.

Raised ponds can be a major source of pleasure to the disabled, as indeed can the whole patio area, if designed to appropriate specifications. The ideal height for working a pond or raised border from a wheelchair is 60 cm. Physical handicap varies enormously, of course, but the comfortable reaching distance of an occupant of a wheel-chair is generally about 60 cm too. So the width of a raised bed, if accessible from one side only, should not exceed this width, which is more than ample. A raised pond or bed which can be reached the whole way round can be doubled in width. A pond 120 cm wide could be 194 cm in length (Kepler's 'Golden Measure') or more, a size which should satisfy the enthusiasm of most patio gardeners.

In order that a wheel-chair should have access to all parts of the patio, no space should be less than 90 cm wide, and where a turning space is required the minimum is 120 × 120 cm. Circular beds or ponds, or curved corners, are less trouble to negotiate than are right-angles. Steps must, of course, be avoided. Gentle slopes made of concrete, ideally no steeper than 1:12, should be

Barbecues

As regards the siting of a barbecue, the usual recommendation is that it should be placed in a sheltered area which is least exposed to the prevailing wind. In windy areas this may be of particular importance, but there are other considerations which you may think deserve priority. Depending upon where you intend eating your barbecue meals, you might well decide that the barbecue would be better placed in a *more* exposed position if

The impact of this design depends upon two interlocking circles, one raised, rather than any combination of plants.

that means the smoke is *carried away* from the dining area. Another point to consider is the convenience of the barbecue in relation to the kitchen. If only occasional use is to be made of the barbecue that may not be important, but if you are frequently carrying trays of kitchen ware past shrubs, or making your way round a fountain or pond, then you might well wish you had chosen a different place for the barbecue.

The final choice of materials, the shape of your pond, the style of a fountain sculpture, may all be, in the final analysis, a matter of taste, but I hope this chapter illustrates how much design is a question of providing practical answers to the challenge of using space effectively. Make a scale drawing of your design if at all possible. No matter how rough and ready your draughtsmanship, the very process of making a plan will throw up all sorts of ideas and options. Moreover, a plan should highlight problems you might otherwise have overlooked. Finally, take your drawing to the site and using lengths of rope, or flour shaken from a paper bag, mark out the boundaries of pond, fountain, beds and walls. Look at what you have laid out from many angles, walking round and about all the elements you intend building. Get the feel of the site, visualise what you have planned, think of any problems they raise and modify your plan accordingly.

Of all the gardening activities, design seems to me to be the one which should least be rushed. The human mind is a peculiar thing, hopelessly perplexed one day, full of answers the following one. Where those answers come from is often a mystery, but how they are obtained experience makes clear: they are obtained by mulling over, thinking, and thinking again about the project in hand. Who was it who said film scripts are not written in Hollywood, they are *re-written*? The saying could well be applied here: successful patios are not designed — they are re-designed.

12 Diary of a pond in progress

If I look back and ask myself why I chose to make a patio and pond, several reasons come to mind. A simple, practical one was that I became utterly tired of stepping out of the porch and on to mud. But that was a small point as compared with the pleasure I had had from water gardening over many years, and which I wanted to continue. The seclusion and low maintenance of a patio appealed to me no less than the attraction of ornamental water. The combination seemed ideal for dealing with the area immediately outside the new house. Besides, the house could only be improved by the addition of these elements. These were the thoughts that filled my mind. There were snags and difficulties to be encountered on the way, as snags there must always be, but these tended to fade as the project took shape. Entries from a diary recall the progression from mud patch to patio water garden:

November 2 It has been an utterly dismal day, with rain almost all day long. I stood at the window this afternoon watching the mist rise in the fading light. The clump of stones that the last owner regarded as a rockery is absurd-looking. It has almost been taken over by the patch of uneven grass that served as a lawn, and this looks as if it has fed giant moths. The patio slabs to the right are not badly laid, but three lines stretch to nowhere in particular and relate to nothing at all. They are a hotchpotch of plain concrete and exposed aggregate. I imagine they were left over from some building project. Nothing could look less appealing at any time of the year. I made a resolution that I would not let another season pass without having tackled it. The whole lot will have to go, but what should replace it?

November 5 I was on the 'phone to Michele this morning, at her office, and the conversation turned to the house she was buying. 'I am doing my own conveyancing,' she said, 'and I am not happy about it.' That puzzled me. 'It's like a doctor treating himself and his family,' she went on. I had never thought of that. The remark gives me comfort. It's years since I designed a pond for myself, and I find that no plan comes immediately to mind.

November 8 While standing at the window before breakfast, lost in thought, my hands thrust in my pockets, Audrey appeared and read my thoughts: 'Looking at it won't change it.' Then she added: 'Nor reduce that paunch you are always complaining about.' That did it, as soon as I got home in the evening I sat myself down by the fire and set to with pencil and paper. After about twenty minutes I had a fair heap of crumpled paper piling up beside me. But at least a few ideas had emerged. I decided to bound the patio with a low brick wall, so that it should be a completely self-contained, formal unit distinct from the rest of the garden. Extending along most of the length of the three walls (the house would make up a fourth wall) should be a raised bed. At a convenient point nearest the kitchen, I put in a barbecue. At 800 mm the wall will be high enough, I reckon, to create the impression that the patio is indeed a self-contained unit, but low enough to avoid casting unnecessary shadows. It is a suitable height for the barbecue too. So far so good, but where to place the pond? If I put it on the right-hand side, it will get the maximum amount of sun. But space is limited there because the porch extends out in to the patio. On the other hand if I put it on the left-hand side, it is going to be shaded for part of the day by the chestnut tree. The chestnut is due, overdue, for what tree surgeons like to call a 'haircut'. That would help; but what decided me was that we would want to sit round the pond and to see it from the sitting-room. That meant the left-hand side.

November 9 This evening I turned my sketch into a scale drawing. From a plain rectangular pond flush with the patio, which was my original idea, I played round with the idea of having two interlocking raised ponds, with water going from one to the other by face masks. The more I thought about the idea the more I liked it. The coping round the higher pond would make a good seat, especially as it would be near the barbecue. The only problem is that a raised pond, consisting as it does of a double wall, is deceptive in the amount of space it takes up. The problem is compounded by having two ponds. I have put down provisional dimensions of 1000×1600 mm for the smaller pond and 1800×3000 mm for the larger. That leaves plenty of room to walk round them, 1 metre at the narrowest point, much more between the house and the pond.

November 11 I decided to tot up my material requirements and nearly stopped when I reached 3000 bricks. Much expense could be saved by dispensing with the idea of having a double boundary wall and making it a single one instead. The piers, there are no less than seven, could be reduced in size from six bricks per course to four. But the result would not be the same. The wall would look thin, the piers meagre. I shall press on.

November 18 Any person of even average intelligence would straightaway accept that paving some 67 sq. metres is done most economically with concrete slabs, and anything else, considering the size of the area, borders on insanity. Yet the temptation to visit the local quarry 'just to see what they have', as I persuaded myself, was difficult to resist. Indeed impossible. I set off this afternoon. No sooner had I arrived than I fell for a light, sandy coloured limestone slab and bought a set on the spot. The proprietor, a kindly, sensible man, quickly noting that I was not clad in exotic Eastern dress but looked singularly like any other impoverished local, did his best to put me off. 'Look,' he said while examining a row of the slabs, 'the colour is by no means consistent.' 'All the better,' I replied, 'that makes them look all the more natural.' I just had to have them.

November 27 Work has begun. I marked out the foundation area with stakes and builder's line. As the evening closed in I took up my place at the sitting-room window and gazed out at the area. Even the builder's line indicating the enclosed area makes the site look better. It cheered me up.

November 28 Having a spare hour this morning I staked out the area for the ponds and walked round and round it in circles, first in one direction and then in the other, until even Cliff (our Jack Russell terrier) was bemused by my antics. But it is essential that one feels satisfied with the space round a pond.

December 14 In a perfect world, everything would be done in its proper time in relation to everything else. The foundation should be laid before the arrival of the bricks. Otherwise the bricks will have to be moved round the corner of the house, then moved again. Thanks to the weather, I have not as much as dug the foundation. Sometimes I get the impression that every cloud from all over Europe converges on this garden.

114

December 18 My patience finally ran out. With the rain simply pouring down – and a good part of it finding its way down the back of my neck – I at last got the foundation dug. I like the size of the patio. It will not be so large that it will require a lot to fill it, nor so small as to appear cramped.

December 20 Nothing is more easily overlooked than the time required to shift materials on to site. No lorry of any size, certainly not one with a hydraulic crane, can negotiate our narrow drive nor pass under an over-hanging laurel. The pallets of bricks are left at the gate. This means the bricks must be brought up the hill, painstakingly, in barrow loads. I spent four hours doing just that today and still have several hundred bricks left. Nearly three hundred paving slabs will have to be moved in the same way. Should I ever get to see the pyramids, I shall appreciate them.

January 6 Was there ever a January like this? The sun beams down at us from a cloudless sky. We work in our shirt sleeves. In fact Jim, who has some experience as a boxer as well as brickie, works stripped to the waist. I comment on the speed with which he can lay bricks (of which I am rather envious). 'Well it's like this,' he said, looking as authoritative as his nineteen years would permit, 'you develop a rhythm to your work and then you work up that rhythm, just like boxing.' He is right, of course, but he might have added that being paid per number of bricks laid has also something to do with it.

January 11 The idea of having a motif set in the bricks appeals to me. I had the words *Sursum Corda* – Be of Good Cheer – inscribed for the pond in town, so why break a good tradition? If a water garden is not cheering, it is a failure. I went down to see Gerard Glendon, a stone engraver, to see what he could do for me. He says he can get me two chunks of white Portland stone which he will bevel and engrave. I think the idea appealed to him. It must be a change from inscribing tombstones.

January 15 The wall rises before our eyes and the raised beds are now complete. There is one hitch. Jim has filled his piers with bricks. 'Didn't you notice that we filled the other piers with rubble?' I asked him. 'Piers made throughout with bricks are stronger,' he replied, adding for good measure, 'There is always some bricks which are marked or chipped that you can't use elsewhere.' He has a point, though it is obviously more economical to use rubble mixed in with a little mortar. But the real problem is that we shall now be short of bricks. That means going to the trouble of fetching some more from the far side of the city.

January 16 Building the ponds has taken a little time. But the additional care is well repaid if you end up with the top of the ponds absolutely level. We laid the Butyl rubber in place yesterday; the odd shape of the larger pond involved much adjusting of the liner (a liner made up to the precise shape rather than a sheet would have been a distinct advantage). Eventually, after carefully checking that all was well, I took courage and snipped away the surplus with a pair of scissors.

January 17 A red letter day, we all stood round the pond in absolute silence, listening to the gentle gush of water from the hose pipe, watching the Butyl lose all slackness as we topped up the pond. It was very satisfying to watch the water rise exactly level with the top of the liner the whole way round.

January 27 I had invited old Michael, the gardener from next door, to see the work in progress and he arrived during his lunch-break today. We were carrying out the final levelling of the enclosed area. 'Going to lay the patio?' he asked glumly. From Michael's conversation you would believe that nothing was possible in this world (though his own garden is perfect evidence of just what is possible). I nodded. He was silent for a moment, then he said: 'Where is the gully trap?' 'We are not going to have one,' I replied. Michael's expression changed abruptly. He no longer looked glum. He looked aghast. 'No gully trap?' he repeated, 'Is it a swamp that you are after?' 'Won't be a swamp, Michael,' I said gaily. He muttered something about the 'younger generation', gazed at the scene with dismay for a few more minutes then wandered off.

January 29 I have no idea when our house was originally built, but the front wall winds to an extraordinary degree. It is a tedious business cutting the slabs to shape and we spoilt more than one. But these can be cut smaller and used at other points. For this reason it is always wise to leave the small sections till last.

February 8 It was raining this morning when I woke up as it has not rained in two weeks. As soon as I was dressed I immediately went out to examine the patio. The pitch, the absorbency of the slabs, and the drainage offered by the gravelly subsoil all proved perfectly equal to their task. The gutter round the porch has, as yet, no barrel. Instead the rain was simply cascading down on to the patio and running out through the main entrance. Water was lying in one place only and no sooner had the rain stopped than that small pool disappeared. To my delight, just before lunch, I heard footsteps on the drive and recognised them as belonging to Michael. He surveyed the scene for a moment. Then he said: 'You won't get heavier rain than that,' and he actually smiled.

February 15 I should never have guessed at just how much bliss there is in walking over dry paving slabs. It seems ridiculous now

how long we tolerated the mushy strip of lawn that intervened between the porch and the garage. In winter it inevitably meant damp shoes, hot tempers and muddied carpets. No man, I am reliably informed, ever learnt to wipe his shoes properly on entering a house. Be that as it may, I am certain no dog ever learned to do so. And I suspect that I got blamed for a great deal of the mud the dogs brought in, but that is now a thing of the past.

February 23 A sudden fall of snow during the night completely blanketed the patio. The effect was pristine except for the two ponds which looked like two black gashes in a pure white carpet. The sight was rather unnatural and weird. If the ponds contained even a few plants, such as *Typha* and Sweet Galingale, whose foliage remains conspicuous, though quite dead, during the winter, the empty, desolate appearance of the ponds would be removed. It was not long before Sophie, our young labrador, was scurrying around in the snow in ecstasy. She had never seen snow before. Within minutes the patio, far from looking fresh and radiant in the wintry sun, had turned to the dirty, wretched grey of slush. But I am consoled at the thought of what effect such antics would have on a conventional garden. By lunchtime all the snow and slush had evaporated except for the shadowy areas not exposed to the sun.

February 28 I noticed how much the soil in the raised beds has sunk over the last few weeks; the result, no doubt, of the heavy rain and the snow. As time is a problem at present I shall probably not plant them up until the autumn. By then the soil should have thoroughly settled. In the meantime, we shall put in annuals to provide some colour during the summer. It will take time for the red brick to lose its new look and tone down. It is rather intense at present. And there is rather too much brick exposed to view. I intend growing a selection of bushy plants in the raised beds, *Hebe* in particular, which will hide the wall behind. Fuchsia too will serve the same purpose and, of course, we intend growing several varieties of *Hedera*. As they grow up the walls and down the troughs the whole patio garden will be mellowed.

March 8 Spring, at last, has arrived. The bright sun, the smell of damp earth on the breeze, the antics of the blue tits and sparrows carried out with renewed vigour on the bird table, the buds showing through on the chestnut and beech, all raised the spirits. I took a walk down by the river in the afternoon and spent a pleasant hour wandering through the beds of Flag, their bright green 'swords' emerging in vast numbers in the boggy area around the river. The Marsh Marigold too has started into growth. They seem to favour the shelter of the many willows that almost form a wood at one point. There the Marsh Marigold grow in profusion, indicating that they thrive in dappled shade, a point worth remembering. I am looking forward to planting up the ponds.

March 12 I called in on David today and to my surprise found him in the middle of his large pond, dividing lilies. It seemed far too early. He held up three or four tubers to reveal emerging leaves. I said I would prefer to wait until the leaves had developed. He then threw a tuber on to the bank at my feet. 'Try that,' he called out, 'If it fails I'll stand you any drink of your choice; if it survives and flowers then the drinks are on you.' He chuckled confidently. The lily is 'Solfatare', which I do not have.

April 20 Messing about with water is one of the joys of childhood. For some that joy never departs. I had a grand time today planting my lilies and marginals. In addition to 'Solfatare', I have *N*. x *Marliacea* 'Albida' and *Laydekeri* 'Purpurata' in the lower pond. 'Albida' is a little too vigorous for my pond but it will be all right for a single season. In the top pond I put the old reliable 'Helvola' and *pygmaea* 'Alba'. In fact I had several tubers of 'Helvola' to hand so I put another pot in the lower pond. Four lilies will be too many when they get firmly established, but I can always transfer them elsewhere when the time comes. For marginals I have about four pots of *Caltha palustris*, one of the small white form which I grew from seed; several *Iris sibirica* in varying hues of blue; one pot of *Cyperus longus*, a variegated Flag and a nice creamy and green striped *Glyceria* which will add colour. And to add a sense of height to the top pond I have put in a pot of *Cyperus alternifolius*. With a few centimetres of water over its crown it should be quite safe from any late frosts. Although all the plants are still small their effect was instantaneous. The ponds no longer look like blank spaces but have come alive with greenery and growth.

April 24 It would have been nice to have had the oxygenators settled in by now, although I rather doubt if the low temperatures we have had lately would have let them develop. Anyway, Rosemary allowed me to root out all the *Myriophyllum spicatum* that I wanted from her pond, and I returned home with a great mass of it. It filled a fifth of the lower pond, if not more, and that is all to the good. The top one contains *Elodea canadensis*.

April 29 A disastrous event took place today that I should have anticipated and so avoided. In the morning I lifted a paving slab, close to the pond, which had been rocking a little; and I put fresh mortar under it. Then sometime in the late afternoon I happened to walk past the pond and something made me do a 'double take' at the fish. It must have been the curious, lugubrious movement of one of the smaller goldfish. It soon became apparent that something was wrong. All the fish were listless and did not dart away at my approach. It was evident that they were all ill. I was at a total loss to understand why until I noticed a vague but tell-tale scum on the surface of the water. Then I recalled the work I had done in the morning. It had been exceptionally windy and I had left a bag of cement near the pond. Some of the contents must have been blown in. I quickly removed all the fish and placed them in a tank. I then completely drained the pond and refilled it immediately. It shows how potent is even a small amount of lime.

May 3 Sadly, two of the six fish died, but the others have fully recovered. None of the plants has been set back. The lime was probably not strong enough to affect them anew and the water was only polluted for a few hours.

May 10 It has been a glorious day, barely a cloud in the sky, nothing stirring in the still air, hardly a sound except the ambient murmur of fish rising to the surface, a robin marking territory from the chestnut, or a chaffinch calling to its mate in the *Escallonia*. I sat by the pond for a quiet half hour. The lily pads have risen to the surface, the Marsh Marigold are in full bloom, the *Glyceria* has stretched up, as has the Umbrella plant. Only the *Pontederia cordata*, which I added the other day, and the Sweet Galingale have made little progress. But they are always slow to start.

May 15 With the amount of sunshine that we have been having over the last ten days or so, the water in the ponds quickly turned green. Nothing can be seen in the depths, not even the goldfish unless they are very close to the surface. Michael came in to see the progress. He looked around and seemed impressed until he approached the pond. He then looked decidedly glum. 'What's happened to that?' he asked. 'It's the growth of algae,' I replied. 'Hmm. It's going to smell some-what', Michael said, shaking his head, 'Aren't you going to clean it out?' I explained

that the underwater plants would take care of the algae and so the colour in due course. 'Starve the algae?' repeated old Michael in disbelief, 'First I ever heard of that one.' Like a fool, when he pressed me, I committed myself to a date, declaring that it would be as clear as crystal by the end of the month.

May 30 'Well, what did I tell you?' said Michael as he looked into, or more precisely, at the pond. ''Tis greener than it ever was.' I had to admit that it was indeed greener. There was no denying it. 'It may take a little longer,' I pleaded, rolled up my sleeve and delved down in the water to pick a few pieces of *Myriophyllum*. Sure enough the tops were light green for several centimetres, a sure sign of growth. All was well.

June 5 The water appeared to have cleared very slightly about three days ago. Then this morning when I went out to the ponds, they were perfectly clear, so clear in fact that you could read a watch if placed on the bottom. I called Michael over the wall. In he came, only to gaze in disbelief for some moments. Then he looked me straight in the eye. 'You've changed the water,' he said triumphantly.

June 7 I sat by the pond after supper and noticed how well the lilies have developed: all have leaves rising and unfurling as they reach for the surface. I am amazed at how quickly a pond fills up with inhabitants. I counted two water scorpions busy diving in search of food. It is said that they can drown if they cannot crawl on watery ladders to the surface, so poor is their swimming ability. These scorpions seem to be doing well enough. I found a caddis larva complete in a superbly made case. Tiny grains of sand formed a good part of the case, but the main constituents were bits of pine needles, still fresh and green. Why pine should be favoured, I cannot imagine, it is not available in every pond and its long, narrow shape must be inconvenient for house building. I noticed too a black leech, ominously snaking its way from one clump of weed to another. They are, however, harmless.

June 8 John gave me a ring today to know if I had any lilies in bloom. I had to admit that so far I had only a few buds. He has had blooms since the beginning of the month. My tubers may be younger than his and I suspect the chestnut tree, despite its haircut, may be delaying the plants a little.

June 11 At last 'Helvola' has bloomed. The first bloom opened a day or two ago. It was joined by a second today. It is surely among the daintiest of water lily flowers, that delicate shade of yellow, the small pointed petals, its starry shape. Margaret came in with her little daughter, Sarah, for afternoon tea. Sarah was enthralled with the pond. First she counted all the fish, and when I told her there were five, not four, she stalked round the pond, turned her head first to one side and then the other, looking under the lily pads until she spotted the missing one. Then she demanded to know the names of all the lilies. On tip-toe, for she barely reached the coping of the top pond, and craning her neck she looked at the starry Helvola bloom. Her face lit up with satisfaction. 'Beautiful,' she said to herself. This would have been around three o'clock, I knew by the gathering clouds that the temperature would drop quite soon and the bloom would close. 'Now if you wait patiently, until after tea,' I said to her, 'That lily will close up and go to sleep.' 'Go to sleep?' she repeated in wonderment. 'You wait,' I repeated. Every few minutes after that Sarah tip-toed over to the pond and, holding her breath, sneaked a look over the top to see if the lily had gone to sleep. I presumed the tip-toeing was for fear of waking the little plant. Eventually her patience was rewarded. 'It's asleep!' she shouted out to us, quite forgetting not to wake the plant. Then remembering herself,

she put a finger to her mouth and in a stage whisper asked: 'When will it wake up?' 'Tomorrow morning,' I told her, picking the bloom, 'if you put it in water and make sure it gets the sun.' She took the bloom in cupped hands, her eyes wide with delight. Perhaps a gardener was born today.

June 16 I was sitting inside listening to the lunch time news with the window open when I heard the faint sound of splashing. I went to the window expecting to find a stray dog lapping at the pond. Instead, the two Shubunkins were in the process of mating, dashing round the pond at great speed. Every now and again, such was the enthusiasm of the pursuit of the male, that both he and the female were breaking the surface of the water, hence the splashing. With luck we shall have some tiny fry shortly.

June 19 This has been a day of days, barely a cloud in the sky and all the warmth of a June day at its best. I spent half an hour or so weeding the larger of the two raised beds. It brought to mind my efforts, eventually defeated, of trying to keep the old rockery clear of grass and weeds. It takes very little time to deal with a raised bed. James and Catherine arrived about midday. I turned on the face masks and as we had our drinks we enjoyed the refreshing tinkling of the water. Lunch, consisting of steaks and a mixed salad, was served from the barbecue; the smell of cooking wafting across the patio had given us all wonderful appetites. After lunch I opened the sitting-room window and put on some favourite 'goldie oldies', Piaf, Layton and Johnstone, George Brassens and many more. Their voices echoed across the patio as we finished the wine, lying in the blazing sun.

June 23 I think the ponds are at their height today. Three of the *sibirica* irises are in bloom, the *Cyperus*, the striped Yellow Flag and *Glyceria* will grow yet higher but not more pristine. Most satisfying of all, each of the water-lilies is in bloom; indeed 'Albida' has no less than three perfect flowers. 'Solfatare' has two and so has 'Helvola'; *Laydekeri* 'Purpurata' has one. Only *pygmaea* 'Alba' shows no sign of flowering. I suspect the tuber is too small and it may take another season before it is ready. When I was on the 'phone to John the first thing he asked was how 'Solfatare' had fared. He had not forgotten our bet.

July 5 It may be no more than imagination, but I fancy that clouds are never so white and billowy as in July. At any rate I never noticed their beauty so much as I have done this year. Whatever way the light falls, the pond seems to reflect the large, floating clouds of July. I had full intentions of finishing an article this afternoon, but instead I wandered out to the pond and gazed at the reflections. The water was unmoving. At one corner a single tall and elegant *sibirica* still held a splendid bloom, and stalk and petals were perfectly mirrored in the surface. I observed the cycle of growth and decay in the *Laydekeri* lily which had one bud emerging, one high above the surface in red and radiant bloom, and one in decay, neither opened nor closed, but sinking below the surface never to reappear. Between the *Iris pseudacorus* and the Galingale I watched a busy spider silently spin a web. That too showed up in reflection in the water, the silvery silhouette of the strands being highlighted by the sun behind. A pond skater, seemingly attracted by a small area in the corner, held my attention for some moments until he or she made a skilful dash across the water to disappear behind the mildewed leaf of a Marsh Marigold. It is a pity the leaves do not remain lush and green throughout the summer. I meant to take my own advice and have a rota of potted marginals to replace those going out of flower. It would be nice to have some *laevigata* or *kaempferi* to follow the *sibirica* irises.

July 10 A diary is the right place for making a confession. In *Water Gardens* I wrote that Fantail Goldfish strut around like fat duchesses. I have now to confess that I have met a duchess only once and that was while trespassing on an estate. She was not fat, rather to the contrary, she was exceedingly thin. But she did, undoubtedly, strut around the garden. So perhaps it is not unreasonable to assume that fat duchesses do the same. I bought two Fantails in town this morning. It may simply be the movements they make with their flowing finnage, but I fancy their temperament is different from plain goldfish.

July 20 This was to have been the opening night of the patio pond. Instead a sudden storm kept us all huddled indoors. However, Peter, gallant to the last, braved the elements and cooked the steaks on the barbecue. We all agreed that food cooked outdoors, especially on charcoal, is more succulent even if eaten indoors. At dusk I switched on the underwater lights which I had placed beneath the face masks. They looked splendidly ghoulish.

July 25 There can be few more pleasant ways of spending a few idle minutes between commuter traffic and supper than at the edge of a pond, especially a pond with fish. Watching their graceful movements as they wend their way through the foliage or rise for food is a fine antidote to city driving. All the fish are now quite tame and I daresay one of the larger and more intrepid goldfish may take food from my hand in time. The Shubunkins are equally tame, the Fantails almost fearless, while the three Golden Orfe tease themselves, like children, by coming forward slowly and then dashing back. What happened to the fish fry I wonder? If any hatched I have not seen them. What I should have done, of course, was to put the mating pair into the upper pond and then returned them to the lower. That way the fry would have been segregated from their elders.

August 15 The last month of summer, and growth is now mingled with decay. Some of the lily leaves are yellowing, and I pluck them off before they sink below the surface. But the lilies, especially 'Helvola', are still blooming well. The variegated iris has lost its conspicuous cream stripes which have merged with the green. The *Pontederia*, however, has come into its own, and the blue bristle flower is now fully open. One does need quite a few plants, nevertheless, to make a show. Otherwise the single bloom, consisting as it does of many tiny flowers which do not all open together, looks slightly tatty. Water mint, which I have added to the marginals, is an excellent late-flowering plant. The lilac whorls are most conspicuous and the plant will thrive under almost any conditions.

August 24 We get few balmy nights in this part of the world, but last night was certainly one. I sat up late reading, and about one o'clock took a walk out on the patio. The moon, which was almost full, was directly opposite the house. I walked to the pond to catch its reflection. Nothing moved in the utter silence. The marginals were casting long shadows across the coping of the ponds or on the patio. The arching branches of Galingale were catching the moonlight and glistening weirdly. A single terracotta pot, newly placed on the pond's edge, looked like a find from ancient times. The lines between the pavings were strikingly defined by the strange light. Suddenly a fish rose with a faint sound in the lower pond and then I noticed some business going on in the far corner.

121

Closer inspection revealed that it was the spider dealing with some prey. There was a slight mist rising which gave the whole patio an aura that was both elusive and spectral. I had never seen it like this before. It was quite some time before I turned in, the scene firmly implanted in my memory. I shall not forget it.

August 28 Paradoxical though it seems, the fish are now less tame at the end of summer than they were at the beginning. The reason, however, is quite simple. The underwater plants have grown with vigour. The fish now prefer to run for the ample cover than remain in the few open spaces. I must pull out some of the plants. I remained sitting on the edge of the pond until the dusk and the dew sent me shivering indoors. Before taking a bath, on passing the mirror, I noticed on my bottom three perfect prints of bricks. While I was seated I felt nothing. Such is the power of a pond over mind and body.

September 10 Autumn is upon us, and as the evening shadows lengthen and come earlier, so the temperature drops perceptibly. We savour the last few days in which we can have coffee or lunch outdoors. I could not guess how many hours we have spent on the patio during the past few months.

September 28 I have been musing on what to add, what changes to make in time to come. There will be many more plants to add to the pond, the raised beds to be planted up, perhaps a trellis to be set against the house and many more terracotta pots to fill. As every gardener knows, a garden, no matter of what kind, is never finished, never complete.

It is always an ongoing project which gains in interest and richness with the passing of the years. I shall spend dark evenings by the fireside musing on the spring to come and thinking up ideas for warmer days.

October 14 The first frost has arrived and, unexpectedly, it has been heavy. What buds remain on the lilies will hardly flower now, though a single 'Helvola' bud struggles to remain upright on the surface. I shall now cut back all the plants, marginals as well as lilies. Some pests hibernate in the stalks of marginals, so it is sensible to cut them back hard, once all growth has ceased. The ponds now look a little forlorn, for all the greenery and colour of the summer is gone. But it is not for long. A few brief months and then, once again, the cycle of new growth and blossom will begin. It is something to which I look forward.

How strange a contrast these few entries would make with what I might have written only a year before. Then I could not look upon the same area without dismay, ragged and unkempt as it was. In a single season the pond and patio became a place to which I turned at every quiet moment. How strong is the attachment one feels for what one has created or lived with day by day. Every gardener knows this experience for himself; but few others can know it. As I now finish this book I would like to think that your backyard, be it full of refuse, disregarded and despised, may yet become a place of enchantment, with fish and plants, water and shrubs; and, more than that, a refuge and retreat from a faster world beyond.

Appendix I: Useful equivalents

Length

2.54 centimetres/25.4 millimetres = 1 inch
30 centimetres = 1 foot
100 centimetres/1 metre = 3 feet 4 inches
1 yard = 0.9144 m

Area

1 square metre = 10.8 sq. feet or 1.2 sq. yards
1 square yard = 0.84 square metres

Volume

1 pint = 568 millilitres
1 Imperial gallon = 4.55 litres
1 U.S. gallon = 0.833 Imp. gallon or 3.785 litres

Weight

1 pound = 454 grams
1 stone = 6.4 kilograms
1 hundredweight (cwt) = 50.8 kilograms
1 ton = 1016 kilograms
1 metric tonne/1000 kilograms = 2205 pounds

Appendix II: Calculation of Areas

To calculate the surface area of a triangular pond, use the formula $\frac{1}{2}A \times B$, where A is the perpendicular distance from the base to where the other two sides intersect, and B is the length of the base.

To construct and calculate the surface area of a polygonal pond, first inscribe a circle, the diameter of which will be the maximum width of the pond. Then divide 360^0 by the number of sides to the pond. For example, if the pond is to be an octagon, eight-sided, then $360^0 \div 8 = 45^0$. Draw a diameter and follow this with a second diameter set at 45^0 to the first. Continue in this way until four such diameters have been drawn. Treat as so many triangles to calculate the area. If for some reason the pond is to have an uneven number of sides, for example 5, then one must use radii at angles of 72^0 and not diameters.

When making a polygonal pond flush with the patio, it is easier to excavate the pond in the shape of a circle. The polygon can be made with the paving slabs. This, however, is only possible if fairly large slabs are being used which will not topple into the pond. In the case of small paving units, it is safer to make the pond itself into the polygon.

The area of a circle can be calculated by using the formula πr^2; where π is 3.1416 and r is the radius.

The circumference of a circle can be calculated by using the formula $2 \pi r$.

To estimate the area of an informal patio or pond, divide the area into squares and average out the fractions left over. Alternatively, peg out with a builder's line the largest rectangle that the area can contain and add to the area of that rectangle an estimate of the remaining areas. This is often a more convenient method than treating the area as so many squares, though it may not be as accurate.

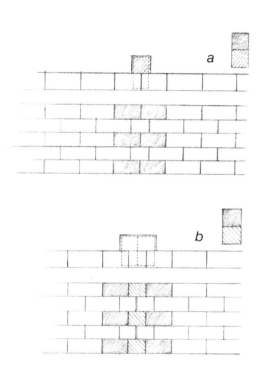

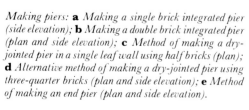

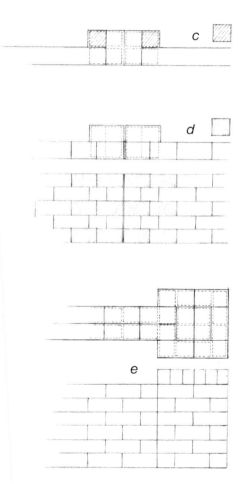

Making piers: **a** *Making a single brick integrated pier (side elevation);* **b** *Making a double brick integrated pier (plan and side elevation);* **c** *Method of making a dry-jointed pier in a single leaf wall using half bricks (plan);* **d** *Alternative method of making a dry-jointed pier using three-quarter bricks (plan and side elevation);* **e** *Method of making an end pier (plan and side elevation).*

Appendix III:

Specifications for foundations, walls and concrete mixes

FOUNDATIONS

The depth of foundations for boundary and screen walls should be, ideally, 450 mm below ground level and resting on stable subsoil. In areas with very severe winters, the foundation should be below the frost line. For raised ponds, raised beds and low ornamental walls the foundation can be laid as little as 150 mm below ground level. If in doubt about the soundness of the subsoil, bed in hardcore.

To determine the width of the foundation, simply multiply the thickness of the wall by three. Again in the case of raised ponds, the foundation will be quite satisfactory if it is twice the thickness of the wall. There will be no tendency for the walls to collapse inwards, but the pressure of water will exert an outward pressure. For this reason the foundation should extend around the outside of the walls.

The thickness of the foundation should at least equal the thickness of the wall or be 150 mm, whichever is the greater.

SCREEN AND BOUNDARY WALLS

Walls up to 900 mm high can be built in single leaf brick or blockwork, 100 mm thick, and with piers 215 mm × 215 mm at 2500 mm centres.

Walls up to 1800 mm high require brickwork or blockwork 215 mm thick, with piers at 5000 mm centres.

MOVEMENT JOINTS

Dry vertical joints should be made at intervals of about 5 metres, if the wall is constructed with concrete bricks or blocks, and at about 10 metre intervals if clay bricks are used.

These figures are appropriate for typical urban situations where some shelter is assumed. In case of exposed areas with excessively high winds, additional reinforcement may be required, and specialist technical advice should be sought.

CONCRETE MIXES

For foundations use cement, sand (fine aggregate) and gravel (coarse aggregate) in the ratio 1:2½:5. If you buy the sand and coarse aggregate already mixed, then the ratio of cement to all-in aggregate, as it is known, should be 1:7.

For the construction of ponds, the ratio of cement, sand and aggregate should be 1:2:3, or 1:4 in the case of all-in aggregate.

For 'lean mix' foundation, suitable as a base for paving slabs, the ratio should be 1:3½:7, or 1:10 where all-in aggregate is concerned.

For in-situ patios and driveways use 1 part of cement to 2 of sand and 4 of coarse aggregate; or 1:5 when all-in aggregate is used.

Note: the apparent difference in the ratios given for the separate materials and for all-in aggregate is more apparent than real. The difference is simply a means of compensating for the settlement which takes place with all-in aggregate.

Picture credits

The author and publisher thank the following for kindly supplying photographs: Alphabet & Image pages 9, 11, 28, 50, 52-3, 74, 78, 93, 98, 112; Blagdon Water Gardens 1, 10, 20, 32, 33, 35, 36 (bottom), 37, 40, 77 (bottom), 81, 96; Cement and Concrete Association 16, 22 (centre), 29, 34, 47 (bottom), 54, 59 (bottom), 60 (left), 111 (top); George Guillemard 14; Jim Horan 22 (left), 61; John Parkhurst 72, 73, 89, 91; Laurence Perkins 99. All other photographs by the author, and all line drawings by Peter Haillay. The author also thanks Penguin Books Ltd for permission to photograph the ponds at Heathrow illustrated on pages 8, 26, 92 and 102.